"A guide for church organizations a [illegible] handbook sets forth well-informed strategies for community-wide partnerships in the fight against modern slavery. *Ending Human Trafficking* includes first-person stories, interviews, and action-step questions to help readers study the issues, understand the ethical concerns at stake, and identify their own appropriate roles in a community-wide model of collaboration. This timely book is a must-read for Christian educators and church leaders who aim to partner with licensed, trained sectors of society—such as law enforcement—with the goal of empowering each survivor's personal dignity."

Karen A. Lee, provost, Wheaton College

"I want every Jesus follower to have their eyes opened to the prevalence of modern-day slavery. *Ending Human Trafficking* does that and so much more. This gripping and practical guidebook gives you, your church, and your family the tools and tips you need to make slavery history."

Kara Powell, chief of leadership formation at Fuller Seminary and executive director of the Fuller Youth Institute

"Wow! A must-read for everyone—regardless of where you volunteer or work. Perhaps the top two taboo topics in the church are mental health and human trafficking. We now have a handbook for becoming what the authors call 'human-trafficking literate.' They guide you through strategies that will help your organization prevent children, women, and men from becoming victims of modern slavery. I was blind, but now I see. Thank you."

Chip Espinoza, author of *Managing the Millennials*

"The world needs more from the church than people who care; the world needs Christians who know what to do. In this compelling new book, Shayne Moore and her colleagues apply this reasoning to the scourge of human trafficking. Their comprehensive, well-informed, and collaborative strategies will empower churches to play their unique and indispensable role in ending modern slavery—effectively helping without inadvertently hurting. Perhaps most importantly, Moore, Morgan, and Yim show how prayerful Christians can make a global difference by protecting the most vulnerable people in their local communities."

Philip Ryken, president of Wheaton College

"*Ending Human Trafficking* is a call to both reflection and action. It challenges the reader to count the personal cost of standing against human depravity and standing up for the millions trapped in slavery. Moore, Morgan, and Yim deploy their substantial understanding and experience to provide a comprehensive guide for effecting real change."

Michael J. Beals, president of Vanguard University in Costa Mesa, California

"This handbook, aptly named, targets a church audience by unpacking the unique ways in which the church can respond to human trafficking. That responsive relevance brings the church into the classroom with well-constructed chapters unraveling the complexities and methodologies of thoughtfully addressing modern-day slavery. Scripture and spiritual values are not thrown in as an afterthought. Faith, as presented, complements an understanding of the complex darkness of human trafficking while turning on a light to strategies of action. The church's sitting down together in reading *Ending Human Trafficking* will multiply their creative conscience on the atrocity of human trafficking. God's people will become a practical and transformational presence to the prayers of millions held in captivity."

M. Christine MacMillan, commissioner, founding chair of the World Evangelical Alliance Human Trafficking Task Force

"In the battle against human trafficking and restoring victims, the church has a vital role to play. In *Ending Human Trafficking*, Moore, Morgan, and Yim provide a well-researched, practical handbook to coach the local church in how to engage antitrafficking collaboratively in their communities and help victims in their recovery. This book offers needed knowledge, best practices in the field, and sound theology. It's a great resource for church leaders, teachers, and ministry students."

Beth Grant, executive director of Project Rescue and author of *Courageous Compassion: Doing Social Justice God's Way*

"I did not know how much I needed to read this profoundly important book! I started reading it in the hope that I could pick up some hints about how to do a better job of motivating well-meaning Christians who feel the urgency but do not grasp the complexities of combating human trafficking. I did not get far into these pages before I realized that I was myself one of those well-meaning Christians who still had a lot to learn on the subject. I hope this book becomes the key resource for a global Christian effort to 'bring liberty to those who are oppressed.'"

Richard J. Mouw, president emeritus of Fuller Theological Seminary

"This book is a gift to the church. It draws a road map that respects and integrates biblical teachings with professional and practical frameworks to bring a collaborative response to build critical safety nets in our communities and nations. It shows the realities of the issues and connects them to the responsibility and the potential of the church to bring hope, healing, and love as fellow collaborators in a broken world. Each one of us is part of this problem, and each one can be part of the solution. Wilberforce said, 'You may choose to look the other way, but you can never say again that you did not know.'"

Helen Sworn, executive director of Chab Dai

"This book is one that has been needed for a long time. It is a comprehensive understanding of the entire issue of human trafficking. The writing is compelling and authored by respected professionals who have been working in this field for a long time. All this is coupled with hope for every person to be a participant in ending this evil."

Jo Anne Lyon, founder of World Hope International

"After reading *Ending Human Trafficking*, I understand more than ever before how Christians, especially churches, are key stakeholders in the fight to combat human trafficking. This book outlines the steps for Christians to see themselves as activists. What I like about this book is that it highlights that the walk to freedom for individuals who are exploited is a *polylithic* one, bringing together the body of Christ. As a survivor of human trafficking, I feel relieved that the church is stepping in to be present and informed on their roles in the dark realities of labor and sex trafficking, so the goals of the Trafficking Victims Protection Act—protection, prevention, prosecution, partnership, and policy—can be achieved. If you are a church, a believer, or anyone who trusts in the gospel, get this book! Use it as a guide on how to support survivors. You will not be disappointed. I will continue to say that it is only by the grace of God that I am alive and able to share my story as a survivor. By getting this book, you are helping give other survivors a voice. As of now, the church is a day too late . . . catch up!"

Bella J. Hounakey, human trafficking survivor-advocate and member of the President's U.S. Advisory Council on Human Trafficking

"I remember feeling unseen by the only place I knew to run to at that time—the church. I was internally screaming for help, and I was confident that they would respond because, well, it was the church. Instead, they gave me water and sent me back with my trafficker. I was confused and angry that they did not do more, but they just didn't know how to help me. I didn't even know that I was being trafficked, so how could they? *Ending Human Trafficking* is a powerful and vital resource that will equip the church with the tools to end human trafficking once and for all. The strategies outlined in the handbook make what seems like an impossible feat feel like a hope-filled journey full of practical steps to fight and defeat such an atrocious crime. The handbook serves as an answer key for ending human trafficking. There is not one agency, ally, or church that has all the tools to end trafficking, but if we put our tools together, we can do it. This is a must-have resource."

Kathy Givens, overcomer and cofounder of Twelve 11 Partners

"I very much appreciated Sandie Morgan's eye-opening presentation on human trafficking at our Crisis Publishing Initiative conference in Hungary in 2017, so I was delighted to hear that she had cowritten a book on this often-misunderstood topic. This practical book delineates the sensible ways the church can most effectively engage in the fight against human trafficking. The compelling overview of human trafficking through the centuries and in all its sometimes-surprising permeations today is well-documented, liberally illustrated with case studies, and theologically grounded. It will be immensely valuable to anyone who is concerned about human trafficking and looking for a way to make an impact in the battle against this evil practice."

Sharon Mumper, president of Magazine Training International

"*Ending Human Trafficking* drew me in with its poignant call for the church to recognize its unique position in addressing the essential work of trafficking prevention. Using principled frameworks and helpful real-life scenarios, this work underscores the importance of conviction and prayer coupled with developing an informed approach for sustained activism that can heal broken systems and invite true freedom."

Betty Ann Hagenau, founder of the Bay Area Anti-Trafficking Coalition and Airport Initiative, recipient of the Modern-Day Abolitionist Award

"When it comes to the prevention of human trafficking, many of us don't know where or how to start. *Ending Human Trafficking* offers churches and individuals valuable insight into the widespread problem of human trafficking and how to be a part of the solution. This book will prove to be a valuable resource for organizations and churches."

Bob Goff, author of *Love Does* and *Everybody, Always*

"Good intentions don't always translate to good impact. While the heart of church leaders to end trafficking is admirable, it's too often the case that a church impedes our shared goal to eradicate modern slavery. This book helps church leaders discover exactly what they need to know before engaging further—and then shows how to take the immediate, practical steps that will make a real difference."

Dave Stachowiak, host of the *Coaching for Leaders* podcast and cohost of the *Ending Human Trafficking* podcast

"Human trafficking—whether for labor or for sex—is modern-day slavery. It is an assault on the dignity of people created in God's image, and Christians must oppose it. In this book, my good friend Sandra Morgan and her coauthors offer a six-point comprehensive strategy for churches to collaborate with others in the godly work of ending human trafficking. This is an eye-opening and helpful book!"

George O. Wood, chairman of the World Assemblies of God Fellowship

ENDING HUMAN TRAFFICKING

A HANDBOOK OF STRATEGIES FOR THE CHURCH TODAY

SHAYNE MOORE,
SANDRA MORGAN, AND
KIMBERLY McOWEN YIM

Foreword by AMBASSADOR JOHN COTTON RICHMOND

ivp
Academic
An imprint of InterVarsity Press
Downers Grove, Illinois

InterVarsity Press
P.O. Box 1400, Downers Grove, IL 60515-1426
ivpress.com
email@ivpress.com

InterVarsity Press® is a resource publishing division of InterVarsity Christian Fellowship/USA®. For information, visit intervarsity.org.

Figure 1: Derek Marsh and Sandra Morgan, Global Center for Women and Justice, Vanguard University
Figure 2: Adverse childhood experiences pyramid, based on illustration by Charles Whitfield, Centers for Disease Control and Prevention, distributed under a creative commons license
Figure 3: Based on research found in James O. Prochaska and Carlo C. DiClemente, "Transtheoretical Therapy: Toward a More Integrative Model of Change," Psychotherapy: Theory, Research & Practice *19, no. 3*
Figure 4: Photo of Manoan kitchen jar, Sandra Morgan, Knossos Palace, Crete

Cover design and image composite: David Fassett
Interior design: Jeanna Wiggins
Images: old cardboard: © fotograzia / Moment / Getty Images
black painted background: © jayk7 / Moment / Getty Images
blue cardboard paper texture: © Nenov / Moment / Getty Images

ISBN 978-0-8308-4187-5 (print)
ISBN 978-0-8308-4188-2 (digital)

Printed in the United States of America

InterVarsity Press is committed to ecological stewardship and to the conservation of natural resources in all our operations. This book was printed using sustainably sourced paper.

Library of Congress Cataloging-in-Publication Data
A catalog record for this book is available from the Library of Congress.

P *25 24 23 22 21 20 19 18 17 16 15 14 13 12 11 10 9 8 7 6 5 4 3 2 1*
Y *43 42 41 40 39 38 37 36 35 34 33 32 31 30 29 28 27 26 25 24 23 22*

WE DEDICATE THIS BOOK TO

the millions of women, children, and men

who are trapped in the evil of modern slavery and

human trafficking, and to those who

work tirelessly to free them.

CONTENTS

FOREWORD

AMBASSADOR JOHN COTTON RICHMOND

HAVE YOU EVER FELT OVERWHELMED by an important task, perplexed about how to take action, or doubtful that your best efforts could make a difference? I have. It is a mixture of preemptive fatigue, profound confusion, and learned hopelessness. The topic of human trafficking can generate these feelings as well-intentioned groups raise awareness about the millions of people suffering in slavery and about the urgency that something must be done. Yet the call to action often seems unclear or unequal to the task.

I think people are willing to draw near to those who are suffering if they believe they can make a difference. For people of faith, there is a clear and unmistakable directive to care for the oppressed and to seek justice. But without a plan, it is hard to put empathy and compassion into meaningful action.

Having spent most of my career on the frontlines of combating human trafficking, I have witnessed this fatigue phenomenon far too often. I saw it when I lived in India working on forced labor cases with International Justice Mission. I saw it as a federal civil rights prosecutor in the United States working sex- and labor-trafficking cases across the country. I also saw it when I led US foreign policy on human trafficking as a US ambassador.

People seeking to combat human trafficking need a guide. Mountain climbers often benefit from guides or Sherpas who have studied the mountain, learned through trial and error, and successfully summited many times. A guide supports the climber and makes the overwhelming task of getting to the top seem possible.

We need guides in our fight for freedom, and this book can help meet that need. The authors have years of experience studying the issues, learning lessons, and overcoming mistakes. They can guide you beyond awareness fatigue and provide a sense of hope that comes from having a practical plan to make a difference.

The authors are calling on churches and faith communities to engage because every victim of human trafficking is created in the image of God and possesses human dignity. When traffickers force their victims to work or to engage in commercial sex acts, they are attempting to deny or diminish human dignity. By separating victims from their traffickers and providing thoughtful, individualized, trauma-informed care, we acknowledge the inherent value of each person. This is faith in action. This is the fulfillment of the Micah 6:8 mandate to "act justly and to love mercy and to walk humbly with your God."

Churches have a unique and special role to play in the larger anti-trafficking movement. There is a great deal of talent within the church. If properly trained and equipped, followers of Jesus stand poised to make a huge impact for good. The church possesses some distinctives that governments do not. Followers of Jesus operate without boundaries. They do not have jurisdictional borders or "areas of responsibility"—they can serve wherever the needs exist. Also, faith communities do not operate for two-year or four-year terms. Short-term thinking is the tainted fruit of bureaucracies. In contrast, some faith communities can think longer term and work through far more flexible funding sources that do not inhibit impact.

A survivor of human trafficking once told me that the only thing her trafficker could not control was her ability to pray. She prayed to God for her pain to end. She prayed that people would do more than be informed and more than merely have distant compassion. She prayed that people would take smart, strategic action that would restore her freedom and allow her to thrive beyond her trauma. God answered her prayers by using his people in many different professions to bring hope.

Within the pages of this book, you will find the information, ideas, and strategies necessary to affect change in the realm of human trafficking. You will learn about the hope-generating importance of prevention, protection, prosecution, partnership, policy, and prayer. Instead of being overwhelmed, you will find inspiration and a practical plan to help restore liberty to those who need it most. As the Scriptures remind us, "It is for freedom that we have been set free."

ACKNOWLEDGMENTS

With profound appreciation and respect, we extend thanks to the women and men who shared their expertise on human trafficking as podcast guests or in interviews. Their professionalism, paired with a heart and passion to end human trafficking, is a model to us and to the world of how we all can collaborate, learn from one another, and effectively fight this evil. This book would not have been written without the many people who shared their stories and experiences.

A special thanks goes to Louise, a survivor whose honesty and vulnerability in these pages are striking. In addition, every guest on the *Ending Human Trafficking* podcast has influenced the content of this book. They have pooled their knowledge to build a better understanding of the complex issues around what it takes to end the exploitation of our fellow citizens in this world. With over 250 episodes in the podcast, there are too many participants to list here, but you will meet many in the following pages. The most notable podcast guests to thank are the survivors who have shared their lived experience and expertise: Holly Austin Smith, Carissa Phelps, Harmony Dust Grillo, Shyima Hall, Stacy Jewell, Rachel Thomas, Bella Hounakey, Rebecca Bender, Amy Rahe, and Kathy McGibbon Givens.

We give thanks for the Global Center for Women and Justice (GCWJ) at Vanguard University of Southern California. We are grateful for their mission of equipping students to address the global status of women and vulnerable populations through collaborative and restorative justice principles, for their vision to develop educational resources to promote best practices and data-driven decision-making, and for serving our communities as a clearinghouse for information on women's issues in a multidisciplinary approach. In 2010 GCWJ board member Dave Stachowiak suggested starting a podcast to reach and educate more people, and in May 2011 the *Ending Human Trafficking* podcast was launched. This book is a direct fruit of GCWJ's mission and vision as well as the podcast's influence.

We would also like to thank GCWJ associate director Derek Marsh, the law enforcement founder of the Orange County Human Trafficking Task Force in 2004 and Sandie's boss while she was serving as task force administrator from 2007 to 2010. Much gratitude goes to another great supporter and podcast subscriber, Ambassador John Cotton Richmond, who consistently models support for others and strengthens connections in the anti-human-trafficking movement.

A special acknowledgment comes from Sandie, who is grateful for her husband, Jean, her best encourager in growing the work of the Global Center for Women and Justice and in life.

Finally, our gratitude belongs to our editors, Edward Gilbreath and Ethan McCarthy, and to InterVarsity Press Academic for being committed to publishing titles that facilitate broader conversations in the academy and the church and for engaging in these most important of issues. Ending human trafficking and working to set free those who are caught in this form of exploitation is one of the most important and urgent issues of our day. We are thankful for the support of IVP to assist the church and the world in fighting this evil with intention, with education, and with passion.

> The King will reply, "Truly I tell you, whatever you did for one of the least of these brothers and sisters of mine, you did for me." (Matthew 25:40)

Introduction

BUILD A SAFETY FENCE

Our task as image-bearing, God-loving, Christ-shaped, Spirit-filled Christians, following Christ and shaping our world, is to announce redemption to a world that has discovered its fallenness, to announce healing to a world that has discovered its brokenness, to proclaim love and trust to a world that knows only exploitation, fear, and suspicion.

N. T. WRIGHT, *THE CHALLENGE OF JESUS*

A STORY FROM DR. SANDIE MORGAN

It was just before lunch when the Department of Justice official who was moderating a conference for human trafficking task force leaders announced it was time to do a table exercise. The topic: discuss one of your biggest task force challenges.

A Texas police sergeant at my table leaned his chair back and laughed. "Easy! The wacko church people."

My colleagues at the table turned to look at me.

As the administrator of the Orange County Human Trafficking Task Force and as an ordained minister, admittedly, I had experienced my own share of well-intentioned yet problematic church people. But this stung.

Our task force co-chair gestured toward me. "Hey, she's one of them."

Trying to defuse the situation, I quipped, "Yes, I can marry you and bury you."

Everyone laughed and the awkward moment passed, but the point was made: in the public square, when it comes to issues of human trafficking, churches and people of faith are often viewed as a problem.

In my own community there are a number of churches that are active in the fight against modern slavery, and not always in good ways. One example is a pastor who led rescue investigations in our community independent of law enforcement, which—needless to say—is incredibly dangerous and irresponsible. He even invited local news media to a rescue. The church members who joined the pastor in those efforts were not police officers or working with law enforcement and therefore could not make an arrest, so the perpetrator got away. Because this pastor had called in the media, the victim's face was now all over the news. These well-intentioned Christians made a bad situation worse. Instead of building trust with their community, they put a victim at risk, compromised and disrupted a large joint law enforcement investigation, and wasted tax dollars.

Another example of misguided yet well-intentioned Christian involvement is the disproportionate focus on sex trafficking over labor trafficking. I know of a group of wealthy white Christian men who, brokenhearted over the sex trafficking situation in Cambodia, traveled to brothels in that country and attempted to rescue girls independent of any government, nonprofit, or church authority. This is the height of savior mentality. At best it is inappropriate and at worst it is nefarious. Sex trafficking of minors is real and horrific and must be stopped. Yet any response to modern slavery must be well-informed, transparent, and carried out in cooperation with all sectors of society.

Another reason Christians are often seen as a problem is their lack of understanding of what is actually involved in fighting human trafficking and modern slavery. One well-intentioned woman who was upset by this evil in her community called me on multiple occasions to tell me about a house that had been left to her by an aunt. She had an elaborate plan to create a restoration home for women rescued from human trafficking, and she planned to staff it with volunteers from her church. Each time she called, I explained that the Orange County Human Trafficking Task Force could not send victims to her home because her facility did not meet state and county requirements. This frustrated her. But instead of being open to learning the proper processes, laws, and guidelines set by state and local authorities, she accused me of religious persecution. Opening rescue homes without proper training and licensing is high risk in our litigious society, and there are ethical concerns around victim dignity and care.

As a Christian leader, minister, and federal task force administrator, I am grieved by the missteps of some of my fellow Christians with savior complexes. I believe strongly that we must be salt and light in the world. But it is essential that we evaluate what this looks like when we are engaging in the fight against modern slavery. As Christians and churches of any size, we cannot go it alone. These convictions have prompted me to reach out and find like-minded Christians, such as my coauthors Shayne Moore and Kimberly Yim, who understand collaboration, who understand how to work across sectors of society, and who are committed to building trust within their communities.

The sergeant's opinion of "wacko church people" who interfere and are problematic is one we have heard repeatedly in our various roles. It grieves us that well-intentioned individuals are harming our Christian reputation as a whole. It is our hope that this book will inform a collaborative and cohesive biblical response in our churches, nonprofit organizations, and ministry efforts. Ending human trafficking will require intentional strategies that equip Christian leaders to respond well to this overwhelming evil.

BUILD A SAFETY FENCE

Imagine a steep and deadly cliff. Today, most churches and nonprofit organizations working in anti-human-trafficking efforts are focused solely on the victims who have already fallen or been thrown off the cliff of modern slavery. The primary focus is on rescue, on scraping up the victims at the bottom. While this is, of course, important, we will never end human trafficking and modern slavery with this as our only strategy. Together, we must erect an impervious fence so that women, men, and children never fall off the cliff in the first place.

If you are someone who wants to help build this fence, this book will educate and assist you and your leadership in discerning what part of it you can build collaboratively with your greater community. What might be your fenceposts? What structural elements can you add? And how can you link your segment to those of others who are also building this protective fence? The following chapters will help you focus your response and resources in wise ways that create sustainable change. Perhaps your community will focus on only one fencepost, such as afterschool care for children in your neighborhood, preventing them from being easy targets for exploitation. Perhaps your church or organization will focus on cybersafety and education, going into schools to do peer-to-peer training.

The safety-fence model is one way the church can be collaborative, partnering with law enforcement and other agencies that fight human trafficking to effectively prevent it from ever happening in the first place. These types of ministries and activities may not be as attention-grabbing or sensational as rescue missions and building expensive aftercare homes, yet it is the only way to end this evil in our time. We must build the protective fence together against modern slavery, creating a force field for the vulnerable individuals who are near the cliff's edge.

It is essential that the church and its leaders study the language and issues surrounding human trafficking and be able to engage in the public square—that they become "human-trafficking literate." Christian communities can build their own fenceposts and ministries to fight human trafficking, but they must be aware, educated, and intelligent about what local law enforcement and social services are doing. For instance, it is necessary to know the laws in our own countries and in nations where we may support nonprofits in this work. Human trafficking is flourishing in our generation, and our safety fence must be strong and strategic.

THE SIX PS

This book is built around the Ps universally used in fighting human trafficking. In 2000 the United States passed the Trafficking Victims Protection Act (TVPA) and the United Nations passed the Palermo Protocol, which generated new global awareness of human trafficking and the need for a common language and education.[1] Both focused on the same three Ps: *prevention*, *protection*, and *prosecution*. These guidelines later expanded to include *partnership*, then *policy*. As Christians, we add *prayer*. Using this globally accepted framework, we can build a comprehensive strategy for the church in our efforts to ending human trafficking.

To ensure the safety and well-being of volunteers as well as victims, we must make sure our efforts are sustainable and follow best-practice models. The TVPA authorized the annual global *Trafficking in Persons (TIP) Report*, which offers guidance for community engagement in anti-trafficking work. This model identifies professional and community roles for an effective response to human trafficking. Every church and nonprofit should make a careful assessment of its expertise and resources to provide a sustainable, consistent, and compassionate response that respects the intersection of public and private roles. When churches engage in the community to work with law enforcement agencies and other secular organizations, they are following a biblical pattern of being salt and light. They are also making wise use of limited resources. One organization or one church may not have the means to set up a residential care facility, but it can provide volunteers and even pro bono professional services, such as counseling or language instruction for international victims.

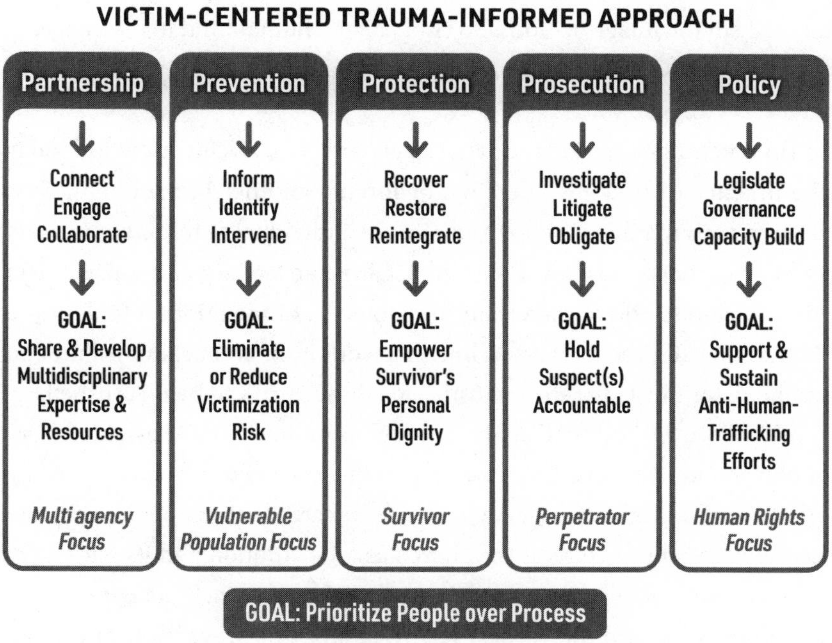

Figure 1. Enhanced collaborative model for human trafficking task forces

Key to collaboration is respect for various partners' expertise and resources. No one can do it all. Prevention requires a comprehensive community engagement plan. Protection entails long-term commitment of significant resources from multiple stakeholders. Prosecution starts when law enforcement recovers a victim and requires coordination with victim service providers. Partnership involves the whole community, which must study the issues, be a voice, and come together to discover appropriate roles. Policy respects wider community guidelines and ensures that trust is maintained. Prayer unites the body of Christ: to one another, to those caught in the evil of modern slavery, and to our God.

THE ROLE OF THE CHURCH: UNIQUELY POSITIONED FOR PREVENTION

Proverbs 31:8 reminds us of our requirement as people of faith to advocate for the marginalized and take action to make things right: "Speak up for those who cannot speak for themselves; ensure justice for those being crushed" (NLT). The theology of *imago Dei* speaks to this mandate. We are all made in the image of God. "So God created humankind in his image, in the image of God he created them; male and female he created them" (Genesis 1:27 NRSV).

Human trafficking and modern slavery are pervasive in our world today. The practice of tricking, coercing, or forcing another human being into slavery steals freedom and joy and robs the individual of his or her identity as an image bearer of God. The church, Christian leaders, and stakeholders with a vision to end human trafficking must be of the mindset to do more than rescue and rehabilitate. While this work is, of course, important and essential, we must also ensure justice for those at risk of being crushed.

We believe the body of Christ is uniquely positioned for the essential work of prevention. When Christians focus on those dangerously close to falling off the cliff, a sense of urgency will rise to catch victims before they are crushed. The very nature of the church as an institution and its placement within communities uniquely enable the church to prevent human trafficking.

Biblically, we see the earliest recorded story of prevention of human trafficking in 2 Kings 4. This story, of a widow at risk of losing her sons to enslavement, contains many factors present in modern slavery, including poverty and the low status of women. We can also connect elements of this story to a sociological theory called "asset-based community development," which strives to build on the skills and resources found within a community and mobilize individuals, networks, and institutions to come together to utilize those strengths.[2] All of these elements are present in our case study from 2 Kings:

> The wife of a man from the company of the prophets cried out to Elisha, "Your servant my husband is dead, and you know that he revered the LORD. But now his creditor is coming to take my two boys as his slaves."
>
> Elisha replied to her, "How can I help you? Tell me, what do you have in your house?"
>
> "Your servant has nothing there at all," she said, "except a small jar of olive oil."
>
> Elisha said, "Go around and ask all your neighbors for empty jars. Don't ask for just a few. Then go inside and shut the door behind you and your sons. Pour oil into all the jars, and as each is filled, put it to one side."
>
> She left him and afterward shut the door behind her and her sons. They brought the jars to her and she kept pouring. When all the jars were full, she said to her son, "Bring me another one."
>
> But he replied, "There is not a jar left." Then the oil stopped flowing.
>
> She went and told the man of God, and he said, "Go, sell the oil and pay your debts. You and your sons can live on what is left." (2 Kings 4:1-7)

By studying this Scripture verse by verse we see a powerful story of prevention unfold. In Old Testament culture, a widow would not have had access to land or other resources that many married women enjoyed. Unfortunately, this is still the reality for widows in many parts of the world today. We know widows and orphans are at higher risk of being trafficked and exploited.

In this story the woman's creditors demand to take her sons as slaves as payment for her debts. This is also a common narrative in human trafficking around the world—an individual owes a debt and must work for others to pay it off. We see it in scams where a smuggler brings someone into the United States from Latin America and now that family or individual owes the smuggler a great debt. Many of the girls rescued in our own communities could tell similar stories of indebtedness leading to their own enslavement. As churches and Christians who wish to help end human trafficking, we begin by asking how it happens in the first place. Exploitation of the marginalized in society is nothing new. It is as old as the Bible.

In 2 Kings 4, two little boys are at risk because their mother is a widow. Likewise in our modern societies, any mother trying to raise children on her own is an at-risk individual. A single mother does not have the same resources as someone in a two-parent home. Her challenges are greater, her vulnerabilities are greater, and the vulnerabilities of her children are greater.

In the biblical story, a religious leader—a "pastor"—gets involved. It is important to look at what Elisha does in this mother's difficult and potentially disastrous situation and compare it to what the modern church might do in a similar situation. A church today might make a video to highlight the horror of human trafficking. Perhaps it would even bring in a victim to tell her story and break our hearts, then collect an offering. In fact, many churches have a benevolence fund for these types of situations.

Maybe Elisha had a fund such as this. He could have said, "How much to pay the debt? Let me write a check." But that is not what Elisha does.

Instead he asks, "What do you have?" He starts with an asset-based approach rather than a needs-based approach. He doesn't base his response solely on what the woman lacks.

The widow answers, "Nothing. Olive oil. A little flask of olive oil."

At this time in history, a little flask of olive oil was just enough to put in her lamp at night to get home safely. It was the equivalent of an AA battery. It was not enough to cook with or to heat her home. Her tiny flask of oil counted as nothing to her, yet it did not matter to Elisha how small it was. She had one resource, and that's what mattered.

When engaging issues of human trafficking and interacting with victims of this horrific evil in our modern context, it is important to learn about vulnerable populations and their communities. We must ask questions to discover what and where the assets are in a given situation. These questions could include: Is she skilled at something? Does she have any vocational skills? Did she go to nursing school? Does she live in an area where she can go to community college? Elisha shows us it is essential to start with what someone has.

After assessing the mother's assets, Elisha makes a strange request. He instructs the woman to go out into her community and borrow empty vessels, empty jars. The ancient prophet not only involves the mother and her sons in the solution but brilliantly pulls in the community as well. This is the second step in ensuring justice for these little boys who are at risk of being sold as slaves. It is essential for the family *and* the community be involved.

Today, we typically think about community involvement as asking for donations and raising funds. If we are going door to door or issuing a call from the pulpit, we ask for checks and cash, not empty jars. If we were in this story, we might have asked the community to give money from their abundance for the boys' deliverance. But that is not what Elisha asks. He instructs the mother to borrow empty jars from family and friends, and in so doing, he engages the entire community.

The next part of the story should fill us with wonder and awe. The desperate woman has been obedient and collected the jars. Now Elisha tells her to shut the door and start pouring from the little flask. In faith, she follows through and offers her small thing—and God shows up. Every single jar is filled. There is not one overlooked jar in the house.

Note that the Bible does not tell us much about the two young boys. We know they are old enough to bring their mother a jar, but we do not know their names. It is interesting to reflect on the idea that perhaps today we sometimes focus too much on the faces and the names of vulnerable children in poverty. While they are indeed suffering, the real story for prevention and change is the parents' story.

Once all the jars are full, Elisha instructs our young mother to take the olive oil and sell it to pay her debts. She does what Elisha instructs, and it's important to note that she is selling something everyone in her community needs—she is not selling a luxury item. This mother contributes to her community as an olive oil entrepreneur, and in her new role she can provide for her sons with dignity.

After this story in 2 Kings we never hear another word about this woman, her sons, or her debts. She has been established as a businesswoman, which has empowered her to care for herself and her children. This outcome illustrates why asset-based development must be a priority in our responses, rather than a focus on needs.

There are many parallels in today's world with this story in 2 Kings. A challenge for leaders and communities who wish to end human trafficking is to look to this story and use it as a biblical model, a prevention strategy to be implemented in our own churches and neighborhoods. Elisha was not simply a social worker who used an ancient version of asset-based community development; Elisha was a man of God filled with the prophetic and empathetic love of God. He did not see this woman as someone to be dismissed because of her lower standing in society, although he could have done so without judgment at that time in history. Instead, he acknowledged the *imago Dei* in her and in her sons.

A long-term sustainable strategy is embedded in this biblical story, one that can be used as a model for partnerships and collaborations in all aspects of combating modern human trafficking. In this story the mother turns to a pastor for help, and he creates a strategy that empowers her. How do we begin to multiply a similar strategy in our churches and organizations to create space for God to work?

Today the church is uniquely positioned to prevent modern slavery because we are trusted in our communities, we have a history of relationship with our communities, and we often have existing facilities, networks, and infrastructure that can be used as assets (for example, buildings can be used for trainings, staging arenas for disasters, and so on). All these thing make the church a valuable partner in local and community efforts. It is important to understand what the church brings to the table, and any effective community assessment will include faith leaders.

Prevention is ensuring that exploitation never happens in the first place. Let's go back to our illustration of the safety fence. Elisha's response of empowering the mother, mobilizing the community, and then God showing up are all fenceposts that prevent the two boys from falling over the cliff of slavery. We have learned that stopping the bad guys is not enough. Rescue and rehabilitation are not enough. We must put people before programs. A biblical model of prevention that empowers a mother to take care of her children, one that empowers vulnerable populations at risk of exploitation, is the best way to avoid modern slavery.

1

ELEMENTS AND TYPES OF HUMAN TRAFFICKING

LAYING THE GROUNDWORK

This is an economic crime. People do not enslave people to be mean to them; they do it to make a profit.

KEVIN BALES

THE MODERN SLAVE TRADE is driven by greed. Like all criminal activity, human trafficking is underreported. It is a complex crime taking place globally and locally, both in organized and systematic ways and erratic and desperate ways. Whether the enslavement of human beings arises from a desperate attempt to provide for one's family or a calculated desire to add millions to a portfolio, profit is the motivation. The demand for cheap labor and sexual services fuels the exploitation of vulnerable people.

There are two major forms of trafficking: labor trafficking and sex trafficking. In both cases someone is being sold to make a profit. The internationally accepted definition of human trafficking is "the recruitment, transportation, transfer, harboring or receipt of persons, by means of the threat or use of force, or other forms of coercion, abduction, fraud, deception, abuse of power or vulnerability, or giving payments or benefits to achieve the consent of a person having control over another person, for the purpose of exploitation. Exploitation includes, at a minimum, the prostitution of others, or other forms of sexual exploitation, forced labor or services, slavery or similar practices, servitude or the removal of organs."[1] Human trafficking also includes "the recruitment, transportation, transfer, harboring or receipt of a child [anyone under eighteen years of age] for the purpose of exploitation," even if other conditions from the above definition are not met.[2]

This definition includes three elements: the act (what is done), the means (how it is done), and the purpose (why it is done). Let's look at each in turn:

- The act (what is done): Recruitment, transportation, transfer, harboring, or obtaining a person for labor, services, or commercial sex acts.
- The means (how it is done): Threat or use of force, fraud, or coercion.
- The purpose (why it is done): Exploitation, involuntary servitude, peonage, debt bondage, slavery, removal of organs. *Or . . .*
- Any commercial sex act involving a minor.

LABOR TRAFFICKING

Often people come to the anti-human-trafficking table because they were told a story about a little girl. In the public imagination, a trafficked person is often a young white female who is taken for purposes of sexual exploitation. But that is actually not the most common form of human trafficking. We tend not to see the images of children working on looms making rugs, young men working in tomato fields, women cleaning up after other people's children, or young boys digging in mines all day for minerals.

Because of the high-profile stories we do hear about, we may be more aware of the significant revenues associated with sex trafficking and the horrific trauma its victims endure. But in studying the problem of human trafficking over decades, we have learned that there are more people trapped in labor trafficking than sex trafficking. Internationally, 64 percent of trafficking victims are in forced labor, approximately 20 percent are in sex trafficking, and another 16 percent are in state-imposed forced labor.[3]

As in sex trafficking, females account for the majority of labor trafficking victims and, tragically, 20 percent of labor trafficking victims are children. There are many types of labor trafficking, with the largest share of victims in domestic work. About a quarter of all labor trafficking is domestic, followed by construction, manufacturing, agriculture, and fishing. Male victims are more likely to be found in mining, manufacturing, construction, and agriculture industries, whereas females are more likely to be forced to work in hospitality and food service industries as well as domestic work.[4]

Bonded and forced labor. There are two general types of labor trafficking: bonded labor and forced labor. The US Department of Health and Human Services (HHS) states, "Bonded labor, or debt bondage, is probably the least known form of labor trafficking today, yet it is the most widely used method of enslaving people." Bonded labor resembles a standard labor contract, but the laborer is rarely able to repay the principal and interest. HHS continues, "Victims become bonded laborers when their labor is demanded as a means of repayment for a loan or service in which its terms and conditions have not been defined or in which the value of the victims' services as reasonably assessed is not applied toward the liquidation of the debt."[5]

Forced labor is when victims are forced to work against their own will under the threat of violence or some other form of punishment. The victims are seen as property and their freedom limited. Domestic servitude, agricultural labor, sweatshop factory labor, janitorial, food service and other service industry labor, and begging are common forms of forced labor.[6]

A number of factors make individuals, especially migrants, vulnerable to labor trafficking. The International Labor Organization explains,

> Although most migration is voluntary and has a positive impact on individuals and societies, migration can increase vulnerability to human trafficking and exploitation. Irregular migrants, for instance, may be subjected to kidnap and ransom demands, extortion, physical violence, sexual abuse, and trafficking in persons. They may start their journeys by willingly placing themselves in the hands of smugglers and become trafficked along the way. Once they reach their destination, migrants who have travelled through regular and irregular channels remain vulnerable to trafficking in persons and other forms of exploitation due to language barriers, challenges of social

> integration, and unscrupulous employers and landlords who take advantage of their limited knowledge of local conditions and reduced bargaining power. Large-scale displacement caused by humanitarian crises such as armed conflicts, natural disasters, and protracted unrest can also create vulnerable populations who can become victims of trafficking.[7]

Labor trafficking predators can be found in all victim demographics, and they exploit any unique vulnerability specific to a victim, such as a developmental disorder, a history of abuse, or cultural beliefs.[8] When employers use force, fraud, or coercion as tactics to control the worker and cause the worker to believe he or she has no choice but to continue the work, the work becomes labor trafficking.[9]

Labor trafficking and modern slavery have been known to flourish in housecleaning services, landscape and gardening businesses, households in which domestic workers are present, large-scale agricultural operations, construction sites, casinos, garment factories, hotels, nail salons, and migrant and transitional communities. Labor trafficking is prevalent in these industries due to the involvement of third-party labor contractors, which have little oversight.

Domestic labor trafficking. "One of the most insidious forms of trafficking—the enslavement of domestics and nannies—occurs under our very noses," write Kevin Bales and Ron Soodalter, authors of *The Slave Next Door*.[10] Often working up to sixteen hours a day, victims in this industry are one of the most prevalent in labor trafficking. They can be involved in cooking, cleaning, childcare, elder care, gardening, and other household work. Trafficked domestic laborers may or may not live in their employer's home. Most victims work for ten to twenty hours a day for little or no pay. In the United States domestic workers can be US citizens, undocumented immigrants, or foreign nationals working under specific types of visas.

Most cases of domestic labor trafficking involve women and girls, but men and boys can be victims too. These trafficked laborers may be forced to endure physical or sexual abuse, prevented from moving about in the community, restricted in their communication with their family and friends, and constantly monitored. They may also be denied medical treatment and experience sleep deprivation.

Fraud is often part of domestic labor trafficking cases as victims are promised false jobs or educational opportunities. They often experience nonpayment, underpayment, or withholding of their wages; visa fraud; and false or altered employment contracts. Coercion may also occur in domestic labor trafficking when victims face threats to family and friends, threats of deportation, document confiscation, and verbal or psychological abuse designed to elicit cooperation. Rachel Thomas, founder of Sowers Education Group, explains, "Psychological coercion is mental manipulation, mind control. Anytime you manipulate someone's thinking in a way that eventually will manipulate their behavior, beliefs, and their whole personhood in a way that is against their own best interests is psychological abuse."[11]

In the United States, 92 percent of domestic workers are women, with 52 percent being women of color. Even though most domestic workers are born in the United States, "they are more likely than other workers to have been born outside the U.S. and they tend to be older than other workers."[12] In a review of reports from the National Human Trafficking Hotline, Polaris reports, "Many victims of trafficking in domestic work are recruited by traffickers and often through family or community ties. Once in the United States, traffickers often use the threat of deportation, as well as document confiscation, to maintain control of foreign national domestic workers."[13]

Immigration status increases the vulnerability of this group as they often hold special visas tying their immigration status to a single employer. "If a domestic worker with an A-3, G-5 or NATO-7 visa leaves an abusive situation, he or she becomes undocumented and risks deportation. Traffickers frequently use victims' unfamiliarity with US laws and customs to convince them there is danger in reporting a trafficking situation to law enforcement or seeking help from social service providers."[14] In addition, domestic work occurs in isolation within the boundaries of a residential home. People in domestic work have minimal engagement with others in the community and can become easily exploited.

There are approximately two million domestic workers in the United States today.[15] Some domestic workers are nannies, house cleaners, and direct care workers for the elderly and people with disabilities. They can be working in car washes, doing landscaping, or working in nail salons. They can be paid directly by private homeowners or agencies or through publicly funded programs or online platforms. Domestic work represents the largest sector of all labor trafficking cases reported to the National Human Trafficking Resource Center.[16]

Below are the types of US visas that are often connected with domestic trafficking. Individuals with these visas arrive via legal channels but are later exploited and enslaved.

- A-3 visa: domestic workers for foreign diplomats
- B-1 visa: domestic workers for certain categories of employers
- G-5 visa: domestic workers for employees of international organizations
- J-1 visa: au pairs

Those of us who want to bring an end to human trafficking can ask ourselves some important questions. For instance, do we know anything about the individuals we hire to clean our homes? Do they speak the same language as the majority of people in our neighborhood? If we are in church leadership, do we know the stories of the people who clean the facilities after regular church hours? Consider taking time to get to know all staff personally.

Servile marriage. Servile marriage is often invisible in a community. It most likely involves a woman entering the United States on a marriage visa who has actually been sold into the marriage. The Orange County Human Trafficking Task Force has encountered many cases of servile marriage. One frequent scenario involves a daughter who is offered through a marriage broker in Southeast Asia. Her family desperately needs financial resources, and a Western client is engaged by the broker. The client visits the potential bride and is provided with photos and supporting documents to apply for the visa. Once the victim is in the United States, she is controlled by threats of deportation or being reported to Immigration and Customs Enforcement (ICE). The victim may refuse rescue because of the risk to her family back home, who has already accepted the money. If a child is born into the marriage, often the perpetrator uses the child as a means of coercion, refusing to allow the child to leave the home with the mother.

In one case we know of, a servile marriage victim asked a neighbor for help after being married by proxy to a developmentally disabled adult male by his businessman brother. The parents had always cared for their disabled son but now were too elderly to manage. Rather than organizing in-home care, the brother arranged a marriage through an illegal marriage broker. The young woman was forced to care for the elderly parents and the disabled son around the clock.

Agriculture. In the United States most workers are protected by the National Labor Relations Act of 1935. This law gives workers the right to organize and protects against unsafe work, guarantees fixed wages, and addresses health issues. This legislation applies to many different types of work environments but not farm labor. Due to reasons steeped in the transatlantic slave trade, history of Jim Crow laws, and Southern politics, farm laborers and household servants were excluded from full rights when this law was passed.[17] This has had a tremendous impact on agricultural work standards in the United States, where competitive prices and cheap labor can quickly lead to forced slave labor.

According to the 2020 US census, there are three million farm workers in the United States.[18] Agricultural workers work long hours for low wages, often in difficult or unsafe environments due to heat or pesticide exposure. Agricultural workers, particularly but not limited to migrant or immigrant workers, are especially at risk for labor trafficking and modern slavery. Immigrants may be lured to the United States with promises of jobs only to be forced into servitude. Many may be trafficked from place to place. Undocumented immigrants are particularly vulnerable to threats of deportation, arrest, and violence. Those with H-2A visas are specifically vulnerable to abuse and coercion, as employers are able to withhold wages, passports, and identification.[19]

It is important to understand how widespread the use of unpaid agricultural workers is in the world, affecting many of the foods we consume. Cases of agricultural labor trafficking have been associated with a variety of goods: tomatoes in Florida, grapes in Italy, sugarcane in Brazil, cocoa in the Ivory Coast, cotton in Uzbekistan—and the list goes on.[20]

The Responsible Sourcing Network is an organization dedicated to ending human rights abuses and forced labor associated with the raw materials found in products we use every day. They have studied the issue of slavery and cotton, finding that "while forced labor remains endemic in many countries, nowhere is it more organized than in Uzbekistan and Turkmenistan, where the governments collectively force over one million citizens to labor in each country's cotton fields every year. The governments shut down schools and public offices for months at a time, mobilize their country's youth, teachers, nurses, and civil servants, and send them to the fields to harvest cotton. They can be expelled, fired, or lose benefits if they do not fill their daily quotas. In China, the conditions are even more brutal. Uyghur and other Turkic minorities in the Xinjiang Uyghur Autonomous Region are forced away from their homes and families to face cultural genocide and work in textile factories and cotton fields."[21]

Mining. Many people might have heard of "blood diamonds" or "conflict diamonds," where people are forced through threats and violence to mine diamonds in Sierra Leone, Angola, Liberia, Central African Republic, or the Ivory Coast. However, some may not be as familiar with the significant problem with human trafficking in the mining of other common minerals. Human trafficking occurs in mining for gold in Burkina Faso, Venezuela, and Peru. In India children are forced to mine for mica, the mineral that provides the sparkle in our cosmetics.[22]

The Democratic Republic of Congo is a beautiful and lush country with a history of invasion after invasion of foreign powers exploiting the natural resources and the Congolese people. Decades of ethnic and political conflict have created large displaced populations in the Democratic Republic of Congo (DRC). This huge central African nation has also faced an influx of migrants, predominantly from its eastern neighbors. The eastern part of the DRC is dominated by dozens of domestic and foreign-backed militias whose goal is to secure control of the mines and trading routes for precious minerals. The DRC is the world's largest producer of cobalt and also has vast reserves of gold, diamonds, coltan, tin, tantalum, and tungsten. Tantalum is the essential semiconductor in all electronics, including aircraft engines and military equipment. Tungsten is the magic that makes our cell phones vibrate. Tin is used as a solder on circuit boards. Gold is not only in jewelry but also in electronics. These minerals are critical components of laptops, smartphones, and other consumer electronics and have created a profit motive for traffickers and militias to exploit vulnerable communities. Consumer demand for cheap electronics drives this.[23]

Child soldiers. Child soldiers are children who are forced to work in any military capacity, whether as a cook, guard, messenger, wife, or slave. These children are abducted, threatened, and coerced. Sometimes poverty drives individuals to join armed groups, while in other cases they join for survival and to protect themselves and their families.[24] In 2019 child soldiers were identified in Afghanistan, Burma, Democratic Republic of the Congo, Iran, Iraq, Mali, Somalia, South Sudan, Sudan, Syria, and Yemen.[25]

Fishing. The global fishing industry is notorious for severe labor abuses and slave labor. From Southeast Asia to Britain and America, there are cases of labor trafficking at all levels of the fishing industry. Thailand has been highlighted in the media as the site of some of the worst slave labor abuses on fishing boats.[26] One investigation revealed that in one year Thai Union Frozen Products, the country's largest seafood company, shipped more than twenty-eight million pounds of seafood-based cat and dog food harvested by slaves to American brands such as Meow Mix, Iams, and Fancy Feast.[27]

In February 2016, President Obama signed the Port State Measures Agreement, which gives officials the power to prohibit foreign vessels suspected of illegal fishing from port access and other services. With this agreement, the United States became the twentieth country to ratify this pact.

> The Agreement on Port State Measures (PSMA) is the first binding international agreement to specifically target illegal, unreported and unregulated (IUU) fishing. Its objective is to prevent, deter and eliminate IUU fishing by preventing vessels engaged in IUU fishing from using ports and landing their catches. In this way, the PSMA reduces the incentive of such vessels to continue to operate while it also blocks fishery products derived from IUU fishing from reaching national and international markets. The effective

> implementation of the PSMA ultimately contributes to the long-term conservation and sustainable use of living marine resources and marine ecosystems. The provisions of the PSMA apply to fishing vessels seeking entry into a designated port of a State which is different to their flag State.[28]

In California, the Monterey Bay Aquarium's Seafood Watch program is preparing to release its first Seafood Slavery Risk Tool. This will be a database to help corporate seafood buyers assess the risk of forced labor, human trafficking, and child labor involved in the seafood they purchase.[29] Information such as this will help consumers know what seafood is ethically sourced and choose products for purchase accordingly.

Manufacturing. Human trafficking has been identified in many forms of manufacturing. From the production of children's toys to soccer balls to garments of all kinds, human trafficking and modern slavery thrive in manufacturing. According to the 2018 Global Slavery Index published by the Walk Free Foundation, $127.7 billion worth of imported garments were at risk of having slavery in their supply chain.[30] Likewise, a US Department of Labor report on goods produced by child labor and forced labor reads, "Labor abuse of children and adults in garment manufacturing occurs in numerous countries from South America to Southeast Asia. From simple T-shirts to luxury evening wear, your clothes may have been cut, stitched, or embellished by an exploited worker."[31]

When shopping, we might ask ourselves why an item is so inexpensive. Was the person who made the T-shirt paid a livable wage? Did the person who made those shoes have the freedom to go home if she wanted?

Restaurants. Many cases of human trafficking have been reported in the restaurant and food service industry. Some of these victims are forced to work as waiters, bussers, kitchen staff, cooks, and chefs with little or no pay. They may be immigrants with legal work visas who obtained restaurant employment through some type of recruiting network. Some victims may be transferred from restaurant to restaurant or rely on their employer for shelter. Traffickers frequently threaten deportation or confiscate documents to control their victims. They prey on immigrants' unfamiliarity with the language, laws, and customs to manipulate or exploit them.[32]

Cocoa. Some of the worst child labor practices are found in the harvesting of cocoa used to produce chocolate. All major chocolate companies are aware of this global problem, and some have made agreements over the years to do better at monitoring their supply chains. In 2001 all the large chocolate companies globally acknowledged the reality of child slavery in cocoa harvesting and recognized their complicity in the problem. These companies vowed to make changes. The official document of this acknowledgment and vow is called the Harkin-Engel Protocol or the Cocoa Protocol.[33] However, since 2001 very little has been done to stop forcing children to harvest cocoa, even though this document has been re-signed and officially discussed in 2005, 2008, and 2010.[34] Miki Mastrati, producer of the documentaries *The Dark Side of Chocolate* and *Shady Chocolate*, was quoted as saying, "Consumers have not been critical enough; they have not asked why a chocolate bar only costs $1 when the cocoa comes from Africa."[35] Even with the creation of the Eliminating Child Labor in Cocoa-growing Communities in Côte d'Ivoire (ECLIC) program,[36] the numbers of child laborers in the cocoa industry rose from 1.8 million to 2.1 million between 2009 and 2015.[37]

One chocolate company, Tony's Chocolonely, has opted to pay a premium of an additional 40 percent for its cocoa in an attempt to provide farmers a livable wage. Tony's is hoping other larger companies will follow suit. Paul Schoenmaker, a Tony's executive, commented in an interview, "Nobody needs chocolate. It's a gift to yourself or someone else. We think it's absolute madness that for a gift that no one really needs, so many people suffer."[38] Consider these statistics:

- The chocolate confectionary business is worth about $100 billion worldwide.
- More than 60 percent of the world's cocoa is grown in West Africa, with Côte d'Ivoire accounting for about half of this.
- The world's cocoa crop is worth about $10 billion per year.
- Forty to fifty million people depend on cocoa for their livelihood. However, many growers do not receive a living wage.

- Child labor is common in West Africa, and about 1.56 million children work in the production of cocoa.
- Instead of attending school, some child laborers work up to twelve-hour days.[39]

When it comes to chocolate, how can we as a church use our consumer power for good? How can we communicate these realities in a clear way that changes consuming habits? What would it take for people to not want to eat someone's else's tragedy?

Organ removal. People in desperate situations become particularly vulnerable to organ trafficking. Both recipients and donors can be distressed enough to try to improve their economic situation or prolong their lives. According to the United Nations Office on Drugs and Crime, while some organ traffickers may profit "solely from criminal trafficking activities, others may be doctors, nurses, ambulance drivers and health care professionals who are involved in legitimate activities when they are not participating in trafficking in persons for the purpose of organ removal."[40]

An example of this type of trafficking involves a woman we know in Pakistan whose husband was working in a brick factory to pay off a debt. When he died, the factory owner came to the woman to take her children as slaves so they could continue working to pay the debt. In an act of coercion, the owner gave the woman a morbid choice. He could take the children forever or she could buy her children's freedom with her kidney. She gave him her kidney.

SEX TRAFFICKING

Sex trafficking is the term used to describe what happens when individuals perform commercial sex or any commercial sex act as a result of the use of force, fraud, or coercion. It is what happens when a child (someone under age eighteen) is given anything in exchange for any sex act or when an adult (eighteen or older) is trapped or forced into commercial sex by someone else. The Palermo Protocol establishes children as a special case for which only two components are required—movement and exploitation—because a child cannot give consent to being exploited even if he or she is aware of or agreeable to being moved. Nearly everywhere in the world laws exist stating that sexual exploitation through the use of force or other forms of coercion is illegal.

Despite increased global policy and media attention focused on the subject, sex trafficking thrives. Sex trafficking is big business, generating billions of dollars in profits each year. It has a profit margin higher than almost any other industry in the world. Experts estimate that although sex slaves account for less than 5 percent of the world's slaves, they generate more than 39 percent of the profits.[41] Due to the lucrative nature of sex trafficking, both small-town criminals and sophisticated organized crime groups have capitalized on this illicit business.

Both international and domestic sex trafficking may involve movement of victims from one country to another, but this is not always the case. Sometimes victims are moved from state to state, county to county, or city to city, or they are not moved at all. Often sex trafficking occurs within the victim's own community.

Victims of sex trafficking can work in what may appear to be traditional prostitution, strip clubs, escort services, brothels, individual homes, massage parlors, pornography, or on the internet. A trafficker closely monitors the victim, choosing clients or rapists, the locations for work, and money. Traffickers may threaten the life of the victim or another family if the victim tries to leave.

Sex traffickers are expert manipulators who prey on a person's emotional or financial vulnerabilities and offer exactly what an individual needs or desires. This manipulation may be perceived as love and care. A trafficker may lavish items on the victim at the beginning of the relationship or may offer shelter and a place to live, money, or a job. The relationship with the trafficker may be violent from the beginning, but more often it starts out positive and eventually becomes abusive. Economic standing, gender inequality, age, family dynamics, and childhood trauma all play a part in the vulnerability of sex trafficking victims.[42]

What once was called prostitution is now commonly and more accurately referred to as commercial sexual exploitation. In cases of persons under age eighteen, it is referred to as commercial sexual exploitation of children, or CSEC. Child sex traffickers are no longer called pimps. Now they are called what they really are: traffickers. This change in language is important as it shifts blame from the victim to the trafficker and to the purchaser of sex, who is a child rapist. These are the people committing the crime—not the victim.

The average age of a person who is first recruited into commercial sex work is fifteen or sixteen years old.[43] Rachel Lloyd is a survivor of sex trafficking and the founder of Girls Educational and Mentoring Services (GEMS), an organization that empowers commercially, sexually, and domestically trafficked girls and women. She explains that a fifteen- or sixteen-year-old is still a child, and even if they claim to be doing these acts of their own volition, laws exist to criminalize sex with a minor. She says, "There's a reason we have age limits and standards governing the 'choices' that children and youth can make, from drinking to marrying to driving to leaving school, and it's because as a society we recognize there's a difference between child/adolescent development and adult development."[44] Children need adults to protect them.

When victims are exploited together, they often form familial bonds with other victims and feel a sense of obligation that is strengthened by the trauma bond of their shared experience in an abusive and exploitative situation. Sex trafficking often generates a cultlike mentality, which can make it very difficult for victims to leave. It's important to listen to those who have survived sex trafficking and value their knowledge and expertise on the subject. When sex trafficking is inaccurately represented in the media and awareness campaigns, it has a detrimental effect on anti-traffickers' ability to recover victims and on the perception of those being trafficked.

REALITY CHECK

Rebecca Bender, Founder and CEO, Elevate Academy[45]

I was trafficked. I met a young man on a college campus. I was a nineteen-year-old single mom trying to put myself through community college. He ended up being a trafficker who took me and my daughter to Las Vegas, Nevada. I was trafficked for nearly six years between three different men.

When I was a young, single mom, my trafficker offered me community and belonging. Toward the end of my exploitation, I lived in a home for three years. There were three other trafficked women and they became my best friends. One in particular was my very, very best friend. We bonded. We spent every day together. We had really similar personalities. We'd laugh and she became that community and tribe that I needed. It was really hard to leave her. She ended up getting sentenced to a year in prison for tax evasion because our trafficker put everything in her name. And that's what kept me there a lot longer because I couldn't leave her behind. I couldn't leave knowing she was sitting in prison, refusing to talk, refusing to tell on me, refusing to put me and my kid at risk. I felt really indebted to stay for her until she was able to get out.

I grew up picturing human trafficking as kidnapped children thrown in a white minivan and taken overseas. When my situation wasn't mirroring that image, I thought I must not be being trafficked. Actually, I thought for a long time I was in a domestic violence situation and so I would call domestic violence hotlines and I would call domestic violence shelters.

I did not self-identify as a traffic victim for a very long time because my situation never matched the brochures, the fliers, the commercials, the media. I think we're doing ourselves a real disservice because I could have stood next to you in the grocery store line and you would not have seen me as a victim of sex trafficking.

My daughter for six years could have been in your kid's class and no one would have noticed. And that is because we are doing a really poor job at marketing this issue. I think as leaders, we have a responsibility with our platform and our reach to ensure that we are telling accurate stories of exploitation to fuel awareness and education and prevention.

I think that mantle of responsibility is important.

Child marriage. Child marriage is any formal marriage or informal union where one or both parties are under eighteen years old.[46] Even though child marriage affects girls most often, boys are also found in forced or coerced marriages before the age of eighteen.[47]

CHILD MARRIAGE IN INDIA

Diana Mao, Founder, Nomi Network; Served on the Public-Private Partnership Advisory Council to End Human Trafficking[48]

According to UNICEF and other data sources, there are about fifteen million child brides married off by age fifteen every year. Twenty-seven percent of girls in India are married off before their eighteenth birthday, and many are married off even before their fifteenth birthday. Those key drivers are what led us to Bihar to combat human trafficking. Another key driver is poverty. Child marriage is more common in poor households, and girls are often married off at a younger age because less dowry is expected for younger brides.

Sadly, girls are not valued in India, especially rural India. Many families consider girls to be *paraya dhan*, which is a term that means "someone else's wealth." Educating daughters is less of a priority than educating sons, who are ultimately responsible for taking care of parents at an old age. Girls are seen as a financial burden, and they are married off at a young age, or even as soon as they are born they are promised to a family to secure their future. Once they reach puberty they are sent off to be wed.

Pornography. When addressing sex trafficking as the church, we must also address the problem of pornography. Just about every book or article that discusses sex trafficking makes a clear connection to pornography. Pornography is often the entry point for being willing to pay for sex. Also, there is a link between what is observed in pornography and what sex purchasers are seeking. After interviewing women in prostitution in nine countries, Melissa Farley, an American clinical psychologist and researcher as well as founder of the organization Prostitution Research, found that 47 percent of trafficked women were disturbed by what the men requested them to do.[49] Eighty percent of commercially sexually exploited survivors report that their customers showed them pornography to illustrate what they wanted.[50]

Pornography is not a world where men and women are equal or where bodies are admired for their beauty. It is a world where women are dominated, urinated on, spit upon, beaten, and raped. "Some scenes are so vile they don't even resemble what we know as sex," writes Victor Malarek, author of *The Johns: Sex for Sale and the Men who Want to Buy It*.[51] Pornography that feeds on dark fetishes such as bondage, pregnant women, animals, violence, and young children is big cyberbusiness. In fact, child pornography is one of the fastest-growing crimes in the United States. In 2015 alone, analysts with the National Center for Missing and Exploited Children (NCMEC) estimated that they reviewed more than 26 million sexual abuse images and that 4.4 million reports were made to its CyberTipline.[52] This problem escalated quickly during the Covid-19 pandemic, when NCMEC saw a 106 percent increase in online abuse reports in one year.[53]

Fight the New Drug, an organization that is raising awareness of the harmful effects of pornography, estimates that 93 percent of young men under the age of eighteen have seen porn, along with 62 percent of young women the same age.[54] These numbers have enormous implications for the church. Church leaders need to make issues of pornography consumption—and its inarguable links to sex trafficking and the sexual abuse of minors—a priority. The church must talk openly about how pornography not only distorts God's will for healthy sexual relationships but also contributes to the evil of sex trafficking. We believe in the *imago Dei*—God's image in all people. But because a screen creates a sense of separation, Christians can be tempted to fall into sin and lose sight of the image of God within those people on the other side of the computer, TV, or phone.

IN SUMMARY

As the church and as church leaders, we must acknowledge that we are part of the problem of modern-day slavery, and we must educate ourselves, teach our congregations, and repent of this reality. As faith communities, we must do more than just talk about human trafficking; we need to actually care about where our products are coming from, how they are being manufactured or harvested, and who has manufactured or harvested them. We must be courageous and honest about the use of pornography in our congregations—maybe even in our own lives—and confess corporately and individually. God-given empathy reminds us there are real people and real families on the other end of our supply chains and screens.

We believe the church is the key to ending human trafficking in all forms. When the church is loving its neighbors locally and globally and caring for those in need in their community and beyond, people are less vulnerable to being trafficked. The church has an incredible opportunity to be salt and light in our world, to model a more connected and intentional way of being a consumer. Understanding the elements and types of human trafficking, along with the part we play, enables the church community both micro and macro to build a safety fence so vulnerable people everywhere never fall into slavery.

BUILDING A SAFETY FENCE: FENCEPOSTS

- Educate leadership and church members about the complexities and types of human trafficking. Practice being able to identify modern slavery in your community and globally. Create sermons and Bible studies focused on labor trafficking and sex trafficking.
- Prioritize bringing the sin of pornography into the light. Confess and repent corporately and individually, provide professional resources for those who need help, and transparently make the connection between pornography and human trafficking.
- Encourage your community to download the US Department of Labor's Sweat & Toil app, which enables people to check whether the products they purchase are linked to slave labor (see dol.gov/general/apps/ilab). That way the next time you order the all-you-can-eat shrimp, you can find out where it is being sourced.

2

PAST AND PRESENT

UNDERSTANDING THE HISTORY OF SLAVERY

The abolitionists succeeded because they mastered one challenge that still faces anyone who cares about social and economic justice: drawing connections between the near and the distant.

ADAM HOCHSCHILD

FOR THOSE OF US ENGAGED in the issue of modern slavery, as with other issues affecting society today, it is imperative to know where we have been and where we are now. Being human-trafficking literate in this way enables us to create strategic and effective ways forward. Knowing and understanding global and domestic historical responses to slavery enables us to critique best practices, create policies, and enact change.

Slavery in all its forms is nothing new. People have been enslaving and exploiting others across the globe from our earliest recorded history. The book of Exodus reveals slavery in Egypt, the New Testament addresses how slaves are to behave, and other historic accounts reveal that civilizations along the Tigris and Euphrates Rivers had ancient forms of slavery, as did Mesopotamia, China's Yangtze River valley, and India's Indus valley. Slavery is acknowledged in the Hammurabi Code, one of the earliest known systems of law. Ancient Greece between the sixth and fourth century had a slave society, and later, in Rome, a third to half of the civilization was dependent on slavery.

During the Roman Empire slavery was so embedded in the culture that it was an accepted part of life. Romans believed they were a superior culture and had a divine right to rule over others. This justified their enslavement of the people they defeated in battle and their belief that some people were born free while others were destined to be slaves. If a mother was a slave, her child, regardless of the status of the father, was automatically born into slavery. Slave labor was used in all aspects of Roman life, with slave laborers often working alongside paid laborers. From agriculture to mining, transportation to education, military to domestic work, and construction to cult rituals, slaves were entrenched in society.[1]

Human trafficking may look different from historical institutional slavery, which is now illegal nearly everywhere in the world, but when we understand this problem in our contemporary time and setting, we see that there are more people enslaved today than there were during the entire transatlantic slave trade. Despite the difficulty obtaining exact data on numbers of slaves, most experts conclude that there are roughly twenty-seven million slaves in our world today.[2] Imagine New York City three times over—all enslaved.[3]

It is important for faith communities to look at our historical connection to institutionalized slavery. Setting captives free from both physical enslavement and spiritual enslavement is at the root of who God is and his heart for his creation. From the Israelites enslaved in Egypt to the Gentiles enslaved in temple worship, God's mission is freedom—freedom from oppression and freedom from sin.

MOSES

In Exodus 34 we see Moses at the top of Mount Sinai, chiseling in stone God's treaty for his chosen people, the Israelites. God has just rescued them from slavery and oppression in Egypt, and he is solidifying his relationship with Israel by providing a visual reminder of his promise to them and hard evidence of his love and character. God is all in with the Israelites, and in return he requires them to be a people set apart and live in a different way from the rest of the world. God's chosen people are to be the light to the world, pointing the world to the good, just, and loving Creator God.

Throughout Scripture we see not only that God cares for his image bearers but that he desires for, pleads with, and commands his people to do the same. Concern for others, especially the oppressed and abused, is a distinguishing factor for God's people throughout Scripture. When God first called Israel as his people, the call came with obligations, responsibilities, and certain standards of living so they could be set apart as God's holy people. Many of these obligations had to do with how God's people cared for the hurting in their community and how they were to engage with outsiders or aliens.

Later in the writings of Moses we learn that God not only wants a people set apart and free to worship him; God also wants his people to be an example of what a free and just community looks like. Throughout all the writings that direct God's people on how they should live, God asks them to take special care of the widow, the orphan, and the stranger—those vulnerable to injustice and without power. In Exodus, God instructs the Israelites to offer part of what they produce to those in need and cancel debts every seventh year so no one becomes trapped in poverty.

God loves his people so much that when they wander, as they are so prone to do, he continues to pursue them by sending prophets to rebuke, remind, and plea for them to live as image bearers—righteous and set apart, reflecting not the culture of idolatry and immorality but the goodness and righteousness of God.

AMOS

The Old Testament prophet Amos came on the scene during the reign of Jeroboam, when Israel was unusually secure politically and economically. God's people had successfully expanded their borders to Solomonic boundaries; however, financial prosperity was manifesting itself in indulgent living. While on the surface Israel looked to be enjoying God's blessing, the nation was morally depraved and corrupt within.[4]

We read in the book of Amos that Amos is sent by God to the people and leaders of Israel to let them know danger is imminent: due to the ways they have made themselves wealthy at the expense of the poor and because of the systems at work in their community that do not offer justice to those who are oppressed, God's wrath will be unleashed.

> This is what the Lord says:
> "For three sins of Israel,
> even for four, I will not relent.
> They sell the innocent for silver,
> and the needy for a pair of sandals.
> They trample on the heads of the poor
> as on the dust of the ground
> and deny justice to the oppressed." (Amos 2:6)

In Amos chapter 5 the prophet reveals that Israel's only hope is in turning away from their sinful ways and turning to God. There is only one way to avoid God's wrath—repentance:

> This is what the Lord says to Israel: . . .
> "Seek me and live." (Amos 5:4-6)

> Seek good, not evil,
> that you may live.
> Then the Lord God Almighty will be with you,
> just as you say he is.
> Hate evil, love good;
> maintain justice in the courts.
> Perhaps the Lord God Almighty will have mercy
> on the remnant of Joseph. (Amos 5:14-15)

At first glance, this might seem simple. The people of Israel know this. Seek God. Seek good. Hate evil. Love good. We can all agree with these very general commands. But then Amos says something very specific: "maintain justice in the courts."

The Bible here is very clear on what is good and what seeking God looks like, and it includes justice in the courts. God's people are set aside to reflect the character of God. They are image bearers, and as image bearers they are called to be holy; they are also called to be just, as God is. God expects his people to seek justice both individually and as a community in order that justice will "roll on like a river, righteousness like a never-failing stream!" (Amos 5:24).

The plea of the prophets throughout Scripture is to warn God's people of his wrath if they do not turn away from corruption and injustice. God's people learn through these prophets that holiness is not just religious rituals or internal beliefs; it is individually and corporately living out the character of God as image bearers.

ISAIAH

In the book of Isaiah, God's people are again called to turn from their rebellion and be restored to right relationship with God. They are to trust only in God, who has promised them a glorious land through Moses and David:

> Learn to do right; seek justice.
> Defend the oppressed.
> Take up the cause of the fatherless;
> plead the case of the widow. (Isaiah 1:17)

Warning of judgment against sin dominates Isaiah chapters 1–39. This is followed by visions of redemption and restoration in chapters 40–66. The specific sins and rebellion Isaiah calls out have to do with how God's people are treating others. God is concerned not with the external rituals in which his people take part but with the injustices they ignore and from which they profit:

> Woe to those who make unjust laws,
> to those who issue oppressive decrees,
> to deprive the poor of their rights
> and withhold justice from the oppressed of my people,
> making widows their prey
> and robbing the fatherless.
> What will you do on the day of reckoning,
> when disaster comes from afar?
> To whom will you run for help?
> Where will you leave your riches? (Isaiah 10:1-3)

When preaching on the following passage, our churches often highlight only the last verse about defending the fatherless and pleading the case of the widow. Our sermons and teachings seldom acknowledge the scriptural context of that verse. The reason God's people are being told to do this is because they have been doing the opposite, and God is angry about it. They are not caring for the vulnerable; instead they are spending their time and resources on meaningless activities and rituals:

Hear the word of the LORD,
you rulers of Sodom;
listen to the instruction of our God,
you people of Gomorrah!
"The multitude of your sacrifices—
what are they to me?" says the LORD.
"I have more than enough of burnt offerings,
of rams and the fat of fattened animals;
I have no pleasure
in the blood of bulls and lambs and goats.
When you come to appear before me,
who has asked this of you,
this trampling of my courts?
Stop bringing meaningless offerings!
Your incense is detestable to me.
New Moons, Sabbaths and convocations—
I cannot bear your worthless assemblies.
Your New Moon feasts and your appointed festivals
I hate with all my being.
They have become a burden to me;
I am weary of bearing them.
When you spread out your hands in prayer,
I hide my eyes from you;
even when you offer many prayers,
I am not listening.

Your hands are full of blood!

Wash and make yourselves clean.
Take your evil deeds out of my sight;
stop doing wrong.
Learn to do right; seek justice.
Defend the oppressed.
Take up the cause of the fatherless;
plead the case of the widow." (Isaiah 1:10-17)

Isaiah warns God's children to turn from their sinful and rebellious ways or the Lord will turn his back on them:

> Woe to the sinful nation,
>   a people whose guilt is great,
> a brood of evildoers,
>   children given to corruption!
> They have forsaken the LORD;
>   they have spurned the Holy One of Israel
>   and turned their backs on him. (Isaiah 1:4)

God has put these same pleas for justice and warnings against injustice on the hearts and lips of prophets in all periods of our history. We have the Ten Commandments, the voices of the prophets, the life of Jesus, and his clear words in the Sermon on the Mount. All these exist to guide God's people to ensure justice in the world for the most vulnerable.

As we are painfully aware, God's people didn't heed the warnings, understand the lessons, or model a just life. More often than we are comfortable admitting, those who claimed to be God's people or followers of Christ perpetuated injustice. This can be seen in the way Christians participated in and profited from the transatlantic slave trade. Many people of faith justified horrific kidnapping, torture, and abuse of all kinds because they believed the lie that if your skin color was lighter, you were better, more holy, and ordained by God to make the world a better place. Even Christian leaders who acknowledged the sin of slavery went along with it for hundreds of years because they underestimated God's power and directive to protect all image bearers, especially the most marginalized. We must look at how easy it can be to be complicit in the enslavement of others.

SLAVERY TODAY

We have the ability to look back and learn from the history of global slavery. Today, individual nations and coalitions such as the United Nations take lessons from the past to create policy and implement laws directed at ending human trafficking. It is important for faith leaders to understand slavery's history, both in the Scriptures and in our own nation's past. It is equally important to understand current legislation surrounding modern slavery so as Christians we can work together with civil society (law enforcement, lawmakers, policymakers, and so on) to help end human trafficking.

A number of national and international legal documents now exist to assist nations in communicating about, understanding, and universally addressing the ongoing global problem of slavery. Two in particular are important for church leaders and anyone else who engages in the fight against human trafficking to familiarize themselves with, because these legal frameworks are foundational both politically and legally in ending human trafficking. These two documents are the Palermo Protocol (United Nations) and the Trafficking Victims Protection Act (United States). Both were created in 2000.

HISTORY OF PALERMO PROTOCOL AND TRAFFICKING VICTIMS PROTECTION ACT

As the US State Department explains, "Human trafficking became a topic of public concern in the 1990s due, in part, to the fall of the former Soviet Union, the resulting migration flows, and the increasing concern about the growth of transnational criminal organizations operating globally. Intelligence reports pointed to sex trafficking and forms of forced labor as some of these organizations' largest sources of profit. The first efforts to address trafficking in persons focused heavily on combating the sex trafficking of women and girls. . . . As the understanding of human trafficking expanded, the US government, in collaboration with NGOs, identified the need for specific legislation to address how traffickers operate and to provide the legal tools necessary to combat trafficking in persons in all its forms."[5]

Human trafficking, like other forms of criminal behavior, is a global problem with many ties to organized crime. For this reason, the United Nations Convention Against Transnational Organized Crime adopted a resolution in 2000 that became the main international instrument in the fight against human trafficking. During a conference that took place in Palermo, Italy, from December 12 to 15, 2000, participants developed an agreement that came to be referred to as the Palermo Protocol. In addition to human trafficking, it targets two other areas of international crime: the smuggling of migrants and the illicit manufacturing and trafficking of firearms. This protocol became a significant step in the fight against transnational organized crime. It created a globally united recognition of the problem and fostered cooperation among nations. The Protocol to Prevent, Suppress, and Punish Trafficking in Persons, Especially Women and Children became the first globally binding document in which specific terms and definitions were agreed on, as well as guidelines regarding cooperation in investigating and prosecuting. The participating countries that signed the Palermo Protocol agreed to protect trafficking victims, cooperate with other countries to eliminate human trafficking, and prosecute traffickers.[6]

The same year the Palermo Protocol was initiated, the 106th Congress of the United States passed its own groundbreaking document called the Trafficking Victims Protection Act (TVPA). The TVPA is a comprehensive law that provides a framework and tools to combat trafficking both globally and domestically. It established the Trafficking Persons Office and the President's Interagency Task Force to Monitor and Combat Trafficking in Persons, agencies that assist in US efforts to fight trafficking and work in collaboration with international efforts. Similar language to what was used in the Palermo Protocol was also used in the TVPA, which helped unify the documents and created a strong foundation for global efforts to eliminate human trafficking.

The TVPA requires the secretary of state to submit an annual report to Congress ranking all global national governments' efforts to combat trafficking, including the United States. The ranking system is a three-tier structure with minimum standards for the elimination of trafficking laid out in the law. This groundbreaking report, called the *Trafficking in Persons*, or *TIP*, *Report*, has evolved over the past twenty years and become an important piece of data in understanding global trends. It includes recommendations for governments to improve their efforts in combating trafficking. Organizations that intersect with anti-trafficking work all use the *TIP Report* as an important resource year after year.[7]

An understanding of these two important documents is essential to understanding how civil and public sectors of society are addressing anti-human-trafficking work. As churches and church leaders intent on building a global safety fence, we would be wise to also understand what our governments are doing—or not doing—in the work of protecting the most vulnerable. In addition, as we actively engage in addressing the problem of human trafficking in our communities, documents such as the *TIP Report* provide real data and information about what is happening in the world. This is particularly useful when we are determining where to give money and resources. Knowing where the work is most effective and where the biggest needs exist informs where we give and where we go—within missions, anti-trafficking organizations, or other nonprofit organizations. Proverbs 18:15 tells us, "An intelligent heart acquires knowledge, and the ear of the wise seeks knowledge" (ESV). Increasing our knowledge around these issues will improve our ethical decision-making.

Also, it is important to ensure that any money a church or individual donates be given to organizations that are following current laws. Because the world has been united around anti-trafficking work for only twenty years, it is possible that at one point there was not a law in a particular country where an organization or church was ministering. However, today there are laws in almost all nations, and the Palermo Protocol applies globally.

Doing our homework and understanding the laws of the land and best practices around anti-human-trafficking work makes us good and faithful participants as well as good and faithful stewards of the resources with which we are entrusted. If an organization asks for money or wants to raise money for an anti-trafficking initiative, it is a good idea to inquire if the organization and its leaders are familiar with the Palermo Protocol, the TVPA, and the *TIP Report*. Do they know the laws in the country where they are serving? If we work and minister internationally, we should be familiar with the Palermo Protocol and other internationally recognized reports, such as the Global Slavery Index[8] and human trafficking reports from the International Labor Organization.[9]

In the United States, any church engaging in anti-trafficking work needs to know and understand the TVPA so it complies with the laws. Churches also need to know what the regulations are in their individual states and counties. Churches often wish to focus on rescuing children, but the laws around children are structured very protectively, as they should be. If you break those laws, you may get arrested and you may get charged with child abuse, child endangerment, or even kidnapping. As Christians and as good stewards, we remind ourselves that the Bible instructs us to follow the laws of the land. We cannot stress just how important this is for church leaders, church members, and volunteers wanting to engage in the work of ending human trafficking.

The United Nations' Palermo Protocol not only outlines the internationally accepted definition of trafficking but also provides a helpful framework. As we've explained, part of this framework is the original three Ps that are globally accepted when discussing and addressing human trafficking: prevention, protection, and prosecution. For the sake of this book and for Christians and church leaders, we address three more Ps—partnership, policy, and prayer.

These Ps—prevention, protection, prosecution, partnership, policy, and prayer—frame this book and help create a structure for how individual faith leaders, communities, and organizations can use best-practice strategies for effective change.

BUILD A SAFETY FENCE: FENCEPOSTS

- Remember as a corporate church body our own nation's shameful history with slavery. Create space and prioritize times of lament and repentance.
- Study the Scriptures in depth, focusing on what God desires for a just and holy people set apart. Explore where we can adjust our own lifestyles and mindsets in order to not have history repeat itself.
- Review with your mission committee the laws of the land in the nations where you are supporting missionaries and nonprofits to ensure you and your organization are following them.

3

PREVENTION

INCREASING SAFETY FOR THE MOST VULNERABLE

The beginning of wisdom is the definition of terms.

PLATO

FOCUSING PRIMARILY ON PREVENTION is the only way to end human trafficking and modern slavery. We cannot stress enough the unique position and importance of the church in local communities in this essential work. There are multiple issues to learn about and consider when embracing the P of protection.

If people are falling over a cliff near a busy picnic area, it seems obvious that someone should build a fence. Prevention strategies predict what might happen and work backward to determine how and where to intervene earlier to stop the sequence. Many factors are involved, including feasibility, sustainability, access, and best practices. This chapter is intended to be a place to begin, not an end. Learn how to identify the risky cliff in your community and where to build a fence.

LEARN THE LANGUAGE

In order to be human-trafficking literate we must learn the vernacular. The church is on the frontlines of vulnerable people's lives given its presence in the community. To work in the space of anti–human trafficking and to collaborate with those who are already doing this work, pastors and church leaders need to know the language. Just as missionaries do not go into a foreign nation and expect people to come to them and learn their language so they will understand the gospel, neither should our churches embark on anti-human-trafficking initiatives or ministries without understanding the relevant terms. When we understand the words and the meaning behind the words, we will be better prepared as we interact with governments, practitioners, and victims. In the public sector, knowing the correct language and being able to use it properly enables church leaders to have access and credibility.

Just as Paul on Mars Hill used the language of the community where he was ministering, Christians who have good hearts and good intentions can be equipped to interact with professionals in the field of anti–human trafficking by using appropriate language. If we lead in the public square with "Christianese" only, we may be misunderstood and lack clarity. In addition, if we cannot use the correct language and hope to work collaboratively, we will be unable to do so because we will be seen as not meeting government parameters. It is our job, our responsibility, to adapt to the language of anti–human trafficking.

For instance, study the laws and language of the state where you reside and learn what occurs when someone is arrested for child sexual assault. Prosecutors may choose to use the most egregious charges with the most significant sentencing guidelines rather than anti-human-trafficking laws that may result in a less severe penalty. It is important to learn the laws in your state, use that language, and learn what tools are available to you and your community.

What we do know about community partnerships is that support of survivors can make a dramatic difference in court outcomes when those survivors are called as witnesses. Derek Marsh said it best in a 2008 video the Orange County Human Trafficking Task Force produced for an awareness campaign. Marsh explained that law enforcement can do its part, but officers don't have all the tools to provide the individual support victims need. A secure and nurturing home for the survivor is important to his or her recovery, but it also assists in cases where victims are willing to testify against the perpetrator. If they are unsure of their future stability, an already difficult court experience will be even more challenging. Often victim advocates and community volunteers make the difference as they walk alongside survivors through the process.

One way to be involved in your community is to come alongside other agencies and fit into what they are already doing to fight human trafficking. In many states the best way to support at-risk youth and potential victims is to become a court-appointed special advocate. Many states have certificates and training programs that prepare volunteers to serve in this way. Learning the language of human trafficking through a secular certification program is an incredible opportunity for church communities wanting to serve on the frontline. In serving, the church becomes salt and light in roles that allow them to respond to needs outside the four walls of the church building.

Sometimes people from a church tell us, "We've been doing this for a long time and we have a support home and we have rescued many kids." But when we do the research, we find the numbers they offer do not match reality. Some organizations and individuals present themselves in hyperbolic terms. In addition, some churches that are attempting to work in anti–human trafficking are utilizing underqualified people. Churches and organizations must do their homework. If we are sending volunteers to serve in professional capacities, some kind of documentation, such as a social worker license or other qualifying certification, is necessary. This is similar to how, when you travel to another country and wish to drive a car, you cannot rent one without evidence of a legal driver's license.

A CASE STUDY

In 2014 a girl by the name of Aubreyanna Sade Parks was picked up by Orange County, California, law enforcement officials. This was shortly after the passing of the Californians Against Sexual Exploitation (CASE) Act, which held that children formerly identified as juvenile delinquents and charged with juvenile prostitution would now be identified as victims. Because of this new law, Aubreyanna was taken to a group home shelter and her trafficker was arrested. Sadly, after a brief stay, Aubreyanna left the group home, and the next morning her body was found with fourteen stab wounds.[1]

When the local newspaper reported the conviction of the trafficker, Aubreyanna was identified as a victim of commercial sexual exploitation of children. Months later, when the newspaper reported another development in the case, the reporter labeled Aubreyanna as a "prostitute." Language matters. We know a child under the age of eighteen is not legally able to consent and does not have personal agency to sell herself. Therefore Aubreyanna, a child, was not a prostitute. Our children are part of our communities, and we need better for them. Aubreyanna was a victim of commercial sexual exploitation, and the courts affirmed that, yet the media and community called her a prostitute. This term changed how the world saw her, and it changes how the community understands sexual exploitation of children.[2]

Language helps us define who the victim is and who the perpetrator is. For most of history, a prostitute has been considered an offender and lawbreaker, and much of the world today still holds this view. This results in stereotypes and moral judgments, and to put that label on a seventeen-year-old who's just getting started in life is wrong. Allowing media outlets to use these labels for victims without thought is also wrong. Aubreyanna was about to graduate from high school. She had already received an acceptance letter from Arizona University. She was a cheerleader. Everybody thought she was going to be successful in life, and yet she was coerced and manipulated by a trafficker and became trapped in that life. The trafficker made threats against her loved ones and, driven by her desire to protect her mother and little sister, she left the group home the night she was murdered.

The language we choose as church and nonprofit leaders to promote our human trafficking initiatives and ministries is crucial. Well-intentioned organizations and churches may use inaccurate terminology that sensationalizes the issue to get attention and pull at the heartstrings of donors. But these stories are happening to real people in real places. How we refer to their experiences must reflect those events honestly and with respect, bringing dignity to the victims.

Language also matters when Christians and church leaders are engaging the greater community, such as when working with law enforcement, social workers, and legislators. Please see appendix A for a full list of terms and acronyms used in these circles. The best way to learn the language is to study the issue.

Many excellent resources are also available through the US State Department Office to Monitor and Combat Human Trafficking, as well as the Department of Homeland Security's Blue Campaign and the Health and Human Resources Trafficking in Persons Office. For a more global language, visit the websites for the United Nations Office on Drugs and Crime (unodc.com) or the United Nations Global Initiative to Fight Human Trafficking (ungift.org). You will also find many opportunities to improve your language skills by listening to the *Ending Human Trafficking* podcast.

BUILD A SAFETY FENCE: FENCEPOSTS

- Train your anti-human-trafficking volunteers in normative language used outside the church with professionals in the field. Encourage church leaders and volunteers to complete government trainings such as those involved in becoming a court-appointed advocate.
- Avoid using "prostitution" language. Use terms such as *sex-trafficked* or *commercially sexually exploited*. Do not use terms that normalize sexual exploitation, such as *sex worker*. Use accurate words such as *abuse* and *exploitation*.
- Use language that reflects our Christian worldview and the view that all people are created in the image of God and are worthy of dignity and respect.

PUSH-PULL FACTORS

Human trafficking is fueled by an insatiable desire for more. It is a big business in which human beings are a commodity to be bought and sold. In fact, the law of supply and demand applies in human trafficking just as it does in the supply chains that turn raw materials into consumer goods. UNICEF explains it like this: "Human trafficking is the only industry in which the supply and demand are the same thing: human beings. People demanding the sale of people."[3] Likewise, author Siddarth Kara explains, "To design an effective response to slavery, it is vital to understand the forces that promote slavery around the world. I believe the most helpful way to frame these forces is in terms of supply and demand."[4]

In modern slavery, the law of supply and demand maximizes profit by exploiting people. There is demand in our world for cheap labor, cheap goods, cheap food, paid sex, child brides, and child soldiers. Understanding the push-pull factors that contribute to vulnerability will help us gain clarity as we create systems of support to prevent it from happening in the first place. Understanding push-pull factors is prevention work, and by focusing on prevention we are swimming upstream and stopping human trafficking before it occurs.

Let's look at an agricultural example to better understand how this economic dynamic is at play. There is a demand in society for plump red tomatoes. There is fertile soil where tomatoes grow, and there are new green tomatoes close to the vine, but the supplier is looking for ripe fruit. The supplier is seeking the tomatoes that hang a bit lower, that are red and heavy and easy to pluck off. In human trafficking situations, vulnerable individuals are the ripe fruit—they are low hanging and easy to find, and there is a great demand for them.

Push factors. The supply side of the equation consists of what we call push factors. Push factors make a person vulnerable to trafficking by pushing them out of the familiarity and comfort of their families and local communities. Both primary and secondary push factors are in play when people become vulnerable to trafficking. Primary factors are things that don't necessarily change and are not in a person's control. Primary factors that increase someone's vulnerability include female gender, young age, widow status, being a single mother, being an ethnic minority, disability, and a history of abuse within the home.

There are very different social constructs shaping the roles of men and women in different countries and in different cultures. Where you are in the world determines how women and men are treated and how they are valued. In 2017, the World Economic Forum reported that women still owned less than 20 percent of the world's land.[5] Land ownership is an extremely important factor for women in their ability to control their circumstances. In the United States we do not usually think about this, as often both the husband's and wife's names are on the deed of a home. But in many other countries, property ownership is driven by patriarchal norms that reduce the power base for women.[6]

In addition, in many countries the preference for sons over daughters has significantly affected the vulnerability of women and girls. The desire of families for male children and the technology available to determine a child's sex before birth have resulted in fewer girls being born. Abortion and infanticide of girls has been on the rise worldwide, especially in areas where sons are favored. Discrimination against women exists before birth, and even if a girl is born, the son preference continues to be a decision-making factor in the home. In places where there is limited access to education, food, or medicine, the son often receives preference.

Take, for example, a family with a daughter who is seven years old and a son who is five years old. An illness begins to spread through the community, and while there is an antibiotic available to fight it, the family can afford only one prescription. In this community where sons are preferred, the five-year-old boy will take priority over his older sister in the family's decision-making process. In another scenario, a family might make the difficult choice to sell their daughter to pay off a debt, not because they want to but because this is a generational pattern. The bottom line is that women and girls are significantly more vulnerable to becoming part of the human trafficking supply in countries and communities where patriarchal norms result in easier access to girls.

Another primary push factor is the status of widows. In many countries, when a husband dies his property stays in his family of origin and does not pass to his wife. The patriarchal line has priority, and the husband's family decides the fate of the wife. In a short amount of time widows can be left with literally no resources. With no options for survival, they become extremely vulnerable to trafficking. According to the United Nations, there are 258 million widows worldwide and one in ten lives in extreme poverty.[7]

Youth is also a primary push factor. The younger an individual is, the less that person's brain has developed, which increases vulnerability to trafficking. Children not only have fewer resources to protect themselves, but they can also lack the ability to make good decisions and consider risk. Consequently, when someone offers them a way out of a horrific circumstance, they are easier to entice. Limited resources and less control over one's own circumstance characterize younger populations everywhere in the world. Add another factor, homelessness, and homeless youth become even more ripe for the picking by traffickers.

Push factors in individuals' lives can compound and become layered. A homeless boy is vulnerable to being trafficked. A homeless girl is more vulnerable. Another compounding push factor is past abuse. When living in an abusive home or experiencing abuse from an intimate partner, a person is more vulnerable to being trafficked because he or she is looking for a way out of a hellish life. This means individuals experiencing abuse can be more easily recruited for trafficking. Abused people desire a safe environment where there is someone to care for them. Those escaping family violence often do so with no resources, and survival becomes their first basis of making choices. Therefore, when someone offers them a place to stay or a way forward in their situation, they may readily accept without skepticism.

Just as gender is a push factor in modern slavery, so is an individual's status in society. Ethnic minorities in most countries are not empowered. There are typically fewer resources, opportunities, and funds available to them, and in many cases they are marginalized in their societies—even persecuted. Their circumstances in their home country can cause them to want to escape to another place where there may be more opportunity.

People with physical or mental disabilities who don't have loving advocates protecting them are easier to manipulate. This may be a child who is deaf or someone with a developmental disability who cannot get the help he needs or understand who he can or can't trust without assistance. Some of the most egregious cases of human trafficking have occurred with this population, and it is one that we as a society must do better at protecting.

People who have been negatively affected by natural disasters such as hurricanes and earthquakes are more vulnerable to being trafficked. In fact, homelessness is one of the top risk factors for trafficking, according to the National Human Trafficking Hotline, which also reports that survivors were recruited by traffickers near shelters or centers offering aid to people in need. Any organization that is responding to a natural disaster needs to be aware of potential human trafficking as it engages in long-term recovery efforts.[8]

Our collective global experience with Covid-19 falls in the category of a disaster and becomes a unique factor in the push-pull equation. During the pandemic we saw unprecedented lockdowns and joblessness. Members of the Public-Private Partnership Advisory Council to End Human Trafficking were inundated with reports of survivors who had lost jobs and were now vulnerable again. A summary is available in the council's 2020 report,[9] which reminds us that any massive-scale health crisis will increase vulnerability.

During the worst of the pandemic, many people said we were "all in the same boat." However, the reality is that we were all on the *same ocean,* but we were in different boats. Our boats were small and uncomfortable, but we had supplies to last through the storm. Many survivors of trafficking were in a boat with no oars, and those who were already at risk became even more vulnerable.

A primary push factor is one an individual has no control over. With secondary push factors, there is more opportunity for intervention. It is important to consider all factors when thinking through sustainable approaches to ending trafficking. Poverty, limited job opportunities, limited access to education, and issues around documentation are typical secondary factors pushing individuals out to the edges of safety where they become low-hanging fruit for traffickers.

Poverty at any level plays a role in vulnerability to trafficking. From having to find food to having enough money for heat in cold weather or finding dependable shelter, the daily work of survival for oneself and one's family forces people to look for ways out of their current circumstances. Without adequate education people are limited to the jobs they are qualified to perform and in growing their daily income. In some agricultural settings, farmers might not have the education to transform their crop that barely supports their family to a crop that is sustainable through different seasons, even in times of drought or heavier rains. Without proper education people are not empowered and do not have tools or resources for self-reliance.

In many places in the world there are simply not enough jobs available, forcing people to look outside their community for work. This often requires the person to move to a nearby city or move across states or to another country. Their circumstances are such that the risk of exploitation in an unfamiliar environment is worth it. When an individual has few resources, assessing risk looks different than it does to individuals with more affluence. What appears very risky to us may not be to the person who has little to lose.

Once someone is on the move, documentation becomes a factor in that person's level of vulnerability. Identification documentation is extremely important both in a person's home country and when a person is traveling. For a variety of reasons, many people do not have proper identification documentation. When someone feels pushed out to find a better life somewhere else, there is often someone on the other side of that decision creating an illegal pathway for them to do so. It is not the movement of people that turns these into trafficking situations; rather it is their exploitation during relocation. If an individual uses illegal means to help someone relocate, this is considered human smuggling. When the person is exploited, it becomes trafficking.

Other factors that push people into vulnerable trafficking situations include war, unstable politics, government corruption, and a general lack of human rights. Anything that creates extreme instability in the local community will cause people to look outside the safety of the familiar and take risks and hope for something better.

Pull factors. A desire for a better life—for achieving one's dreams—is a pull factor. Like a magnet, this hope pulls people toward something that is perceived to be better. Job opportunities, higher standards of living, media messages, and the internet can all pull people into believing that a better life exists outside of their current situation. Pull factors involve victims' hopes and dreams and also market demands.

Pull factors are linked to the demand side of economics, such as the demand for cheap labor and inexpensive goods and services. When we think of demand in the context of human trafficking, we often connect it to sex trafficking only. However, consumers of all kinds of products and services are part of the demand problem. We influence market demand with what we are willing to pay for and for how much. The consumer creates the demand and sets the value of the product or service, whether it involves clothes, cars, housecleaning, food, paid sex, pornography, sex tourism, or adult sex entertainment. We, the consumers, create the demand that sets the supply chain for human trafficking in motion.

When addressing the problem of human trafficking, we need to understand push-pull factors. This may look like educating ourselves about homelessness, unemployment, and family abuse. It may look like ministering to kids who don't have backpacks for school or helping a single mother who is living paycheck to paycheck. In fact, offering a single mother a little assistance can help her avoid child welfare services intervening and taking her kids away. The simple gesture of helping a struggling single mother who doesn't have enough groceries can prevent an entire family system from being vulnerable to trafficking. Giving this kind of support to our communities is being salt and light; it is intervention in a push factor; it is preserving a family; it is prevention.

PUSH-PULL FACTORS IN CHILD-SEX-TRAFFICKING PREVENTION

Research shows that children who are at risk and who have experienced child abuse and neglect are much more likely to become victims of human trafficking.[10] It is important to be alert for children in unsafe circumstances that can put them on a path to further exploitation and even being commercially sexually exploited. The challenge for those combating the trafficking of children is to find an early point in a child's abuse to intervene, which may prevent the child from falling into the hands of predators. Where can you intervene in your community? Supporting young families is a good place to begin.

Consider a scenario where a mother finds herself raising her children alone and is not able to manage. She becomes involved with a man who promises to take care of her and her children. He moves in and begins to molest her young daughter. What if support for the single mother had been a priority to her community? Perhaps she would not have put herself and her children at risk if she could have managed alone. In another scenario, a teen mom is working full time while raising her son. Her brother offers to take care of her two-year-old on Saturday mornings so she can sleep in. Two years later, when her son starts pre-kindergarten, school officials learn that the cartoons he watched all those Saturday mornings were pornography and the child was being sexually abused.

These scenarios are examples of how an abused child becomes at risk of conflating sexual abuse with "love." The child receives attention, and this becomes a grooming experience. For those hoping to disrupt the push factor and prevent child sex abuse, early intervention is key. Informational brochures and warning fliers handed out in middle schools may come along too late in a child's life.

When children reach early adolescence, they experience a growing sense of power and self-determination. This can lead them to run away, thinking they can take care of themselves, only to find themselves with no resources and vulnerable to grooming and exploitation.

Churches are well-positioned to work toward prevention in their communities, which they can do by including the most vulnerable children in their extracurricular activities for children and youth. Do you remember studying Maslow's hierarchy of human needs in school? This social theory describes the human needs we all share. Basic needs of food and safety must be met before we can attain the higher-level needs of esteem and self-actualization. That means when we are helping the vulnerable, we often start with the basics: sandwiches and dry socks and even a place to sleep.

In child development, these needs are described as developmental assets. Do you have any assets? An apartment? A car? These are simple structures that are part of a secure growing-up pathway. Do you belong to a church? Go to a school where your graduation date is known? These social assets are important in healthy child and youth development. When those assets are missing, a child is more likely to experience higher-risk behaviors, because assets are protective. When assets like strong family, community, and church connections are in place, there's less drive to find connection in other places.

The Search Institute is an organization that conducts research on the protective nature of developmental assets and how they prevent risky behaviors. It has created a chart of forty developmental assets that are important in a child's development and growth.[11] These assets fall into two categories: external and internal. It is important that children have external assets at an early age—things like a safe home, a supportive family, and boundaries. Internal assets, such as self-esteem, are difficult to develop without the external framework. That's why it's important to be sure children have food, housing, and safety before we start building self-esteem. In fact, on the Search Institute list, self-esteem is number 38. On Maslow's hierarchy it comes after physiological safety and belonging. Children's ministry leaders sometimes begin with aspirational goals without making sure a child has the basics. The results of the Search Institute's work tell a dramatic story. Youth with ten assets or fewer had much higher rates of alcohol and drug abuse and violence, while youth with more than thirty assets had fewer high-risk behaviors.

What does this mean for church ministries to children? If you wish to do prevention work for children, offer them something to do. We do not want to wait for a vulnerable teen to get picked up by a gang and then sold to provide revenue for that gang, with our response being to start a gang ministry. Instead, we swim upstream and create interventions by providing programs for youth to get involved in before they reach that point.

A church in Yuma, Arizona, that committed to disrupting push factors in their border town between the United States and Mexico has discovered that teaching neighborhood dance can change lives. Sending children to music or dance lessons not only gives them something positive to do, it builds resilience. These children develop new skills and begin to grow in confidence. This empowerment builds assets into their lives. We can avoid the need to rescue by thinking creatively and empowering the vulnerable in our community.

Some children may never become victims if we offer afterschool or other supportive programs. Empowering children and building assets into their lives is about using positive developmental strategies.[12] Students who are involved in sports and afterschool activities have less "hanging out" time, and they are safer and more secure. These programs do not protect them from everything, but when it comes to push factors, they help.

While push factors inform prevention, pull factors need our attention as well. Online recruiting that plays off dreams is a common strategy, as you will learn in Brittany's story.

BRITTANY'S STORY

Tracy Webb, Senior Trial Attorney, Cyber Crime and Child Abuse Policy and Prosecution, Internet Crimes Against Children Task Force, Los Angeles[13]

Not all victims of child sex trafficking are victims of past abuse. Instead, their dreams for their life are exploited and the trafficker plays on this to groom them. Brittany (name changed) is from a happy home; she's twelve years old and dreams of being a model. Her parents consistently say to her, "Not until you finish high school."

She lives in the suburbs of Chicago and has access to the internet, where she meets a man who says he is a talent scout. Brittany is very beautiful and the "talent scout" asks her to send him a few pictures. He doesn't ask for sex pictures. He just wants headshots and other fun photographs. He sends her a burner phone so they can talk when she's not on her computer since her parents make her turn it off at 10:00 p.m.

Eventually he tells her there is a casting call in Los Angeles and that she is exactly what they are looking for. He sends her an electronic plane ticket and tells her a taxi will pick her up the next night at 11:00 p.m. after her family is in bed.

When Brittany leaves the house that night, a cab is waiting for her outside and takes her to the airport. Because she is twelve years old, she doesn't have to have a permission letter to fly alone. Right before she is about to land in Los Angeles, the flight attendant, noticing tears in Brittany's eyes, asks her if she is all right. Brittany admits she has never been away from home overnight alone and begins to share her story.

The flight attendant responds immediately and calls the air marshal, who meets Brittany when the plane lands. Pretending to be Brittany, officers use her phone and text the number of the "talent scout" she has been communicating with, instructing him to meet in baggage claim, where they arrest him.

Eventually, law enforcement figures out the trafficker's IP address, and they go out to a small town east of San Diego. They rescue seventeen children who have been groomed and recruited online just like Brittany.

When law enforcement agents call Brittany's parents, they tell the officers they have the wrong number, believing Brittany is still in her room. Going to check on her, they are in utter disbelief that she is not in her bed.

Brittany was not from an abusive family situation and poverty was not an issue. She was just a young girl with a dream and access to the internet.

PEER-TO-PEER APPROACHES TO INTERVENTION

Many trafficking-prevention materials for adolescents are designed by well-meaning nonprofits to warn against the dangers and then presented to youth by adults. However, youth do not see themselves as vulnerable. We need to understand the nature of the adolescent brain. During this developmental stage, there is more activity in the limbic system, which controls emotions, than in the prefrontal cortex, where risk management occurs. The prefrontal cortex is not fully mature until age twenty-five or twenty-six.[14]

How does this affect the behavior of a youth? Perhaps a parent instructs a fourteen-year-old not to go to the mall alone. The teenager rolls her eyes and says, "Nothing will happen to me," and she goes to the mall with or without the knowledge of the parents.

Often when working with adolescents, adults feel they have done their job of warning youth against trafficking when they hand out fliers and warn against red flags. However, research shows that these tactics have less efficacy than peer-to-peer, youth-led approaches. One frequently cited example is the DARE (Drug Abuse Resistance Education) program designed to reduce substance abuse among youth. A number of studies have reported its ineffectiveness.[15]

On the other hand, an example of a peer-to-peer approach is the Live2Free club at Vanguard University in Southern California, which goes into middle schools and high schools to do prevention training. These college students have credibility with younger students since they are closer to the same age. They teach about how human trafficking affects students and demonstrate apps that engage personal responsibility in purchasing products like chocolate and clothes, which may be keeping people across the world in slavery. These peers share real stories of exploited youth and empower participants by offering opportunities to role play with a friend in a typical high-risk scenario, such as being approached at the mall or on the internet.

This method is based on a combination of anticipatory guidance and a bystander approach. The concept of anticipatory guidance is borrowed from the health-care world. Say an individual goes to the emergency room with a gash on his leg. The doctor stitches it up and the discharge nurse explains when to return to remove the stitches. The nurse goes over a list of possible adverse reactions and what to do in each case: If you have a fever, call this number. If the area around the stitches becomes red and warm, call the doctor. The patient knows what to expect and is taught what to anticipate, hence the term "anticipatory guidance." Role playing in a peer-to-peer approach helps youth identify and anticipate so they can avoid being tricked or lured into an exploitative situation.

The bystander approach decentralizes the conversation. In order to avoid problems with self-identification and victim-centered language, the bystander model instead emphasizes a neutral, peer-led approach. The suspected victim is asked if they might know anyone who fits a given set of criteria that are common to victims of abuse but are not specific to human trafficking. If the victim at this point self-identifies, they may be redirected to the appropriate assistance.

This peer-led approach does not focus on the suspected victim but rather asks, "Do you know someone?" This overcomes the teen invincibility barrier—the belief that "nothing will happen to me" and "I can take care of myself." In this phenomenon, personal disregard for risk causes resistance and leads adolescents to tell the questioner they can take care of themselves. But that same belief does not extend to their peers. Once, during a Live2Free presentation in a juvenile detention facility, many of the young men (ages fifteen to seventeen) wanted more information—but not for themselves. Rather, they stood in line to ask for information for a cousin or a neighbor. They cared about their community.

An especially helpful tool peer-to-peer volunteers can use is a phone number to text when someone needs help. This number is the National Human Trafficking Hotline, which can be reached by calling 888-373-7888 or texting BEFREE (233733). More than 60 percent of the contacts received by the National Human Trafficking Hotline are texts.[16] Many of those texts are victims under the age of twenty-five. When working with youth, offer the referral number so they can share and keep their community safe. Decentralize the conversation—in other words, don't say, "I'm giving you this number in case you're in trouble"; instead say, "If you know someone who might need help, here's a number to call."

PUSH-PULL FACTORS OF POVERTY (BY SANDIE)

My friend could hardly wait to tell me the news. I had arrived at the United Nations to participate in a presentation on human trafficking for the Commission on Sustainable Development when my enthusiastic friend approached me. Two years earlier she and I had spent five days together in Zambia training faith leaders from all over the nation at the Jesuit Center for Research and Reflection. During those training sessions, I taught a case study about a girl I worked with a number of years ago in Athens, Greece. Here is her story.

Maria (not her real name) was seventeen when she graduated from high school in Ukraine. Her father died in a Chechnyan conflict, and her mother and eight-year-old brother depended on Maria to become the breadwinner as her mother survived by doing laundry for other families. The Soviet Union had collapsed and there were no jobs. One day Maria and her best friend saw an ad for an interview for jobs in Greece, and they both eagerly decided to apply.

On the appointed day, they took the bus into the city and stood in line at a beautiful hotel suite with dozens of other girls to apply for the jobs. Maria completed a job application with all of the expected information, including her address and next of kin. During the interview, she shared freely about her family and her hopes and dreams. At the end of the day, she was thrilled to return to tell her mother she had a job. She would be leaving in two weeks and promised to send half of her earnings to her mother and save the other half to attend nursing school.

Two weeks later, Maria met the "travel coordinator" at the train station, where she turned over her legal documents. On the long journey to Greece she dreamed about her adventure and a wonderful future. When they finally arrived at the Turkish-Greek border, the girls were taken inside a building and each placed in a separate room. Maria had barely laid her head down on the pillow when four men dressed in police uniforms (not because they were policemen, but to begin the process of breaking down her trust in law enforcement) entered the room and gang-raped her. She was in shock. A few hours later, a madam came and took her downstairs. Her mouth, wrists, and ankles were duct-taped and she was placed under the false bottom of a little car and taken over the border, where brothel owners were waiting to purchase her.

For nearly twenty-one months Maria was moved every couple of weeks. This kept her disoriented. She could not make friends, and she did not trust anyone. When she no longer cared for her own safety, her captors threatened her, telling her that if she ran away, they knew where her eight-year-old brother lived and there was a market for boys as well.

Maria was eventually rescued along with several other girls who were very sick. The greedy brothel owners had placed all of the sick girls in a bar and called the tip in to authorities themselves. To these traffickers this is their business. They were simply getting rid of faulty products. It was easiest way to get rid of these girls quickly, since it was so easy to obtain more.

Maria's story contains many of the classic elements of human trafficking as outlined in the Palermo Protocol and the Trafficking Victims Protection Act. Her traffickers offered her a job that didn't exist—fraud. They brutalized her—force. Finally, they threatened her little brother—coercion.

While I was at the conference center in Zambia teaching others about trafficking, I shared Maria's story as a case study over and over. The story took on a life of its own. When friends and family would visit the participants at the conference, they would be ushered into the reception area. Someone would come and get me and invite me to tell Maria's story again.

I remember one guest asking me to tell the story yet again, emphasizing, "My daughter remembers every detail."

As I wrapped up Maria's story for the last time at this conference, I had to dash off to catch a flight to attend another conference in another country. I received warm farewells from my Zambian hosts, and this training experience became one of my fondest memories. I was deeply encouraged by the engagement from the participants and their friends and families.

All this came rushing back as I stood in the hallway of the United Nations. My Zambian colleague told me that Maria's story was being told over and over across all of Zambia—at awareness events, in schools, and in churches.

"Sandie, I must tell you how powerful that story is to us!" she exclaimed.

She went on to tell me about six young people from a poor village who were recruited for jobs in Lusaka with the promise of going to school in exchange for a few hours of work every day. Fortunately, they had heard Maria's story and they were smart. They investigated as best they could to find out whether these were real jobs. When they arrived in Lusaka they were taken to a hotel and each given separate rooms, which was not normal.

But they remembered Maria's story.

One boy, recognizing that they were all isolated from one another, explained that the hair on the back of his neck stood up because he remembered that part of Maria's story. It hit him what was happening. This young boy was small, so he was able to crawl out of the bathroom window and he ran to the police station for help. He and the police promptly returned to the hotel, where the officers rescued his friends and arrested the four traffickers.

Maria and these boys were at risk due to poverty and were simply looking for ways to secure resources. An intervention for the push factor of poverty can include ministries and programs around microfinance, education, vocational training, and empowering and enabling individuals and communities to become financially stable.

IN SUMMARY

By understanding the push-pull factors associated with human trafficking, the church is uniquely positioned to create a safety fence supporting and utilizing effective interventions. Some of these fencepost strategies are not glamorous; however, they may be something your church is doing already, such as an afterschool program. This is important prevention work.

BUILD A SAFETY FENCE: FENCEPOSTS

- When people are materially poor, they are vulnerable. Build their resilience against trafficking by working with organizations that address the root causes that make people vulnerable, such as those that provide safe spaces, livelihood support, and skills and vocational training.
- When creating programs for the youth in your church, plan for ways to include all kids in your community, especially those who may have vulnerabilities. Encourage congregants to volunteer at afterschool programs such as Boys and Girls Clubs or YMCAs.
- Partner with local food banks and shelters.
- Explore and create your own peer-to-peer prevention program in your community.
- If a congregant is a teacher and learns about a need a student may have, have a process in place for that teacher to ask for church help to fill that need anonymously.
- Understand the push-pull factors in your own community and in the communities and nations where you minister. Work toward alleviating push factors where you are able.

EXPOSING THE MYTHS OF HUMAN TRAFFICKING

As the problem of human trafficking and modern slavery has grown in public awareness both domestically and globally, many myths and misconceptions have taken root. Below are some of the most common:

- Myth 1: Trafficked persons can only be foreign nationals or immigrants from other countries.

- Myth 2: Human trafficking involves moving, traveling, or transporting a person across state or national borders.
- Myth 3: Human trafficking is another term for human smuggling.
- Myth 4: There must be elements of physical restraint, physical force, or physical bondage when identifying a human trafficking situation.
- Myth 5: Victims of human trafficking will ask for help or assistance and will self-identify as a victim of a crime.
- Myth 6: Human trafficking victims always come from situations of poverty or from small rural villages.
- Myth 7: Sex trafficking is the only form of human trafficking.
- Myth 8: Human trafficking occurs only in illegal, underground industries.
- Myth 9: If the trafficked person consented to be in their situation, then it cannot be human trafficking or against their will because they "knew better."
- Myth 10: Foreign-national trafficking victims are always undocumented immigrants or here in this country illegally.
- Myth 11: "Citizen saviors" can bring an end to human trafficking.
- Myth 12: If it's a statistic, it must be a fact.

Dr. Sandie Morgan, one of the authors of this book, is also a host of the *Ending Human Trafficking* podcast. When she interviewed Derek Marsh, associate director of the Global Center for Women and Justice, they addressed these common human trafficking myths in more detail:

> ***Sandie:*** Derek, your work as a former detective on the police force brought you face to face with these myths. Tell us about myth number one, this idea that trafficked persons can only be foreign nationals or only immigrants from other countries.
>
> ***Derek:*** I can tell you exactly where that myth came from. When we first started searching for grant opportunities, and when the TVPA (the Trafficking Victims Protection Act) was enacted in 2000, the initial focus of that legislation was people being brought into the United States or any country associated with the United States. This was the only focus for funding at that time.

The initial myth started because funding was focused on foreign-national trafficking and people being brought into our country, brought into other countries against their will, or at least being misled and brought there through force, fraud, or coercion. However, that's since evolved, and we recognize now that our domestic minors—our adults as well—can be trafficked within their respective countries, whether it's the United States or any other country.

Sandie: Let's move on to myth number two. This is important because many NGOs set up efforts right at the border, and the myth is human trafficking is a crime that must involve some form of travel, transportation, or movement across state or national borders. What's the reality?

Derek: Many initially funded task forces had either a presence on the border or a presence at an international airport or they had a presence in shipping ports. Today, the federal law is very clear about this: transportation is an element to human trafficking but it's not an essential element to the crime. You can have someone just next door, you can have them in the same county, the same city, in the same house. People are exploited in their homes and never leave their front door. The crime of human trafficking does not always require crossing a border.

Sandie: Myth three is that human trafficking is just another term for human smuggling. Explain this to us.

Derek: Something that can get confusing is the concept of human smuggling versus human trafficking—for instance, the common practice of moving immigrant wives across borders. Human smuggling does cross national borders, which makes it more of an administrative crime. This crime ends at the border. Human smuggling becomes human trafficking the moment that person is taken advantage of, misled, or forced to do things against their will. Paid or not paid, it doesn't matter; transported or not transported, it doesn't matter. This is one of the first things I train folks to understand: human smuggling is an immigration problem for immigration officers on the border, which is a separate issue from human trafficking.

Sandie: Myth number four is there must be elements of physical restraint, physical force, or physical bondage when identifying a human trafficking situation. Many media images out there contribute to the strength of this myth because they show people in handcuffs or wrapped in ropes or with chains all around them. Tell us the reality.

Derek: I agree the images used historically have been very egregious and they have shown people in horrible situations where they are chained, they're locked down, they're in rooms like jail cells where they are unable to leave of their own free will. Not all victims of human trafficking experience anything like those images, but people use them thinking it will make human trafficking easy to understand.

However, I go back to the TVPA. This bill was championed by many non-profits and grassroots organizations. As a result, a lot of examples presented to lawmakers were situations where people were held in physical restraints in places such as Texas, California, Florida, Atlanta, Chicago. This set the stage for people to think human trafficking has to be a crime of force and it has to be something that involves bondage; it has to involve sex.

The reality is different. In fact, we find more often than not that people are not physically restrained; instead they're restrained through threats. They're restrained through believing they don't have any opportunities. Sometimes they're restrained by being made to believe they're actually complicit in the crime, maybe even given money in order to cause them to feel they're partners in the crime. All these techniques used by traffickers get people to do what they want them to do without having to monitor them 24-7, or needing to have them physically restrained. Psychological controls are in some ways more powerful than forcing people through physical bondage or through physical force to perform labor or sex services.

Sandie: That leads to the fifth myth. Myth five says victims of human trafficking will immediately ask for help or assistance and will self-identify as a victim of a crime. Why is this not true?

Derek: Similar to domestic violence where you have individuals, usually women, who learn to live with the abuse, human trafficking victims do not always fight against it. They go with the flow because it's the devil you know versus the devil you don't. It's this idea that they have nowhere else to go and no other opportunities. Often a victim is going to protect her children or other family members because of threats being made.

With human trafficking, domestic violence psychological tactics apply and sometimes more so, especially if you take into account the age of a victim, a person possibly not having language skills, cultural skills, an education, or opportunities to interact with other people from their culture. They begin to speak the language only to those who are holding them hostage. A victim may begin to identify and bond with the trafficker.

In fact, a word we frequently use in training is "hypervigilance." This is when a victim is so worried about what the trafficker is doing that their only focus is on keeping that person pleased. The victim is focused on survival only. Even though they could pick up a phone and call 911, run out the front door and wave down a cop, go to somebody for help, or whatever the case may be, they don't do it because they are in survival mode.

Sandie: That makes sense. Now let's look at myth six, which is that human trafficking victims always come from situations of poverty or from small rural villages.

Derek: Again, I harken back to the beginning of human trafficking enforcement, the TVPA. As a result of that first piece of legislation, many people were represented as living in rural villages with no education, no training, no expertise in anything—poor folks who had no other choice except to come to the United States or a country that had more opportunities, where they were then exploited. Today we're finding victims of human trafficking who do not meet that stereotype. They have bachelor's degrees or equivalents, or master's degrees. Some have been teachers or are professional folks in their countries who choose to immigrate to the United States and then are subsequently victimized.

Sandie: Myth seven is a very common one we hear, and that is that sex trafficking is the only form of human trafficking. But that's just not the case, is it?

Derek: There's a study by a Harvard professor claiming that 96 percent of all trafficking is labor trafficking. United Nations reports claim anywhere from 50 to 70 percent of all trafficking is labor trafficking. If we look at the numbers across the world, labor trafficking is more prevalent than sex trafficking. The International Labor Organization estimates that 60 to 70 percent of all trafficking is labor trafficking.

I believe the myth of sex trafficking prevalence exists because of the fact that historically in US law enforcement, there was funding and training in investigating sex crimes. Many departments have vice units where the focus is on investigating and prosecuting sex crimes. Where there is funding and training there will be more statistics and stories. When we look, we find. Today, globally, we have a more comprehensive understanding of the accurate prevalence of sex trafficking and labor trafficking.

Sandie: Myth eight is that human trafficking occurs only in illegal, underground industries. Derek, what's the reality?

Derek: We have a lot of social media content that is posted, and we have movies such as *Taken*. I can think of ten more movies off the top of my head that have a human trafficking focus. These stories often focus solely on illegal criminal organizations taking advantage of immigrants or domestic victims. These sensationalized stories create a myth, a mythos, that it's all about illegal criminal enterprises.

However, often human trafficking looks like domestic servitude, where individuals victimize foreign nationals, or people in family units being forced to do labor in the home. There are forced marriage examples, and these do not come out of gang activity or vast criminal enterprises. We see human trafficking in the clothing industry given our demand for inexpensive clothing and, again, this is not the result of underground criminal enterprise.

Sandie: Myth nine brings us to a slightly different issue. If the trafficked person consented to be in their situation or was informed what type of labor they would be doing or that commercial sex would be involved, then it cannot be human trafficking or against their will because they knew better. What's the reality?

Derek: This is tricky because people are under the impression that if an individual consents to a situation, for instance prostitution in a foreign country, then they can't claim later to be a victim. The idea is that they should have known better. However, the crime of human trafficking is not what an individual agrees to; rather it is how that person is treated. This is the pivoting point.

A woman may agree to sell her body, but it becomes trafficking when she is held by force, fraud, or coercion. These tactics may include not letting her go out, not letting her eat unless she is told when she can eat, or not allowing her to be in control of her documents. And they do not pay her what they promised.

Another example is that a person may be promised work in a restaurant but when they arrive to work, their identifying documents are confiscated and they are told that they have to work around the clock for no pay or they will be turned in to the authorities and reported to be in the country illegally. This is another instance where an individual initially agreed to a situation, but the conditions changed and now they find themselves a victim of trafficking.

In law enforcement we have seen situations with senior care facilities where people were told they would be paid as senior care workers but that they owed the traffickers eighty thousand dollars for securing the job. In addition, these victims were required to pay room and board. As a result, they could never pay off the debt. They were basically free labor. Traffickers use the cost of bringing the victim into the country to hold them hostage, and now we have a situation of trafficking.

Sandie: Which leads us to the tenth myth, which is foreign-national trafficking victims are always undocumented immigrants or here in this country illegally. What's the reality?

Derek: In the United States, we hear many stories about people coming across the border not properly documented, whether that be in panga boats, tunneling, crossing rivers, being put into awkward positions in vehicles, or other transportation methods that are horrendous. We may be of the mindset people would only do those things if they were attempting to illegally enter a nation. But the reality is a lot of people enter countries such as the United States legitimately through student visas or through work visas. People immigrate to a country and desire to be a legitimate member of society, whether they're visiting or moving for the long term. Refugees and immigrants are especially vulnerable populations in societies and can become targets and victims of human trafficking.

Sandie: More recently, human trafficking has become a hot topic in the media, which is resulting in new nonprofits and NGOs popping up almost every day with the mission to fight human trafficking. This illustrates and leads us to myth number eleven—this pervasive mindset of the citizen savior.

Derek: I will tell you first, before I contextualize the citizen savior myth, that I have never met anyone who, once they truly understood the severity of human trafficking, did not desire to do something about it. This desire, along with an intense emotional response and disgust, results in some individuals reacting without wisdom or sound strategy. Some go beyond the pale, if you will, and this is where we get the concept of a "citizen savior." These are the people who overstep their roles in combating modern slavery, such as conducting investigations independent of law enforcement, conducting interventions without training, interfacing with people on the street or in situations where they believe there might be trafficking, and actually attempting rescues.

This is a big problem. When it gets to the point that individuals or organizations are doing investigations or surveillance, they are now interfering with victims in the middle of their victimization. They do not have the backup or the skill set, and many times they do not have the ability to make a legitimate case or to make a legitimate rescue. Traffickers are ruthless criminals and these activities put the citizen savior and the victim at great risk.

Sandie: It is very complicated, but the bottom line is we need to work with law enforcement and not disregard that we have due process and we have legitimate ways of collecting evidence. If we desire to prosecute and to put perpetrators away and provide justice for victims, we have to work with law enforcement, not perpetuate the myth that we can do this work as lone rangers.

Lastly, myth twelve is the belief that if it is a statistic then it must be a fact. What are your thoughts on this?

Derek: Statistics can be helpful, but the reality is that it is extremely difficult to collect accurate data on illegal activity that happens in the shadows. Those working in this arena keep trying hard to standardize how we as a global community gather statistics and numbers in order to track what is going on. Yet it is a very complex issue that does not lend itself to easy gathering of reliable data. As a result, the numbers presented are not always the numbers that accurately reflect the reality of human trafficking in the world.[17]

When it comes to myths and misperceptions, it's important for pastors and church leaders to model and teach responsible sharing of social media posts and articles on human trafficking. When something is posted to Facebook or Twitter that seems over the top, sensationalized, or highly disturbing, the best thing is not to immediately repost it or share. The wise thing is to fact-check. This is another way the church can be salt and light in the world. Promoting conspiracy theories, even if you think there is some evidence, does not promote God's justice in the world.

BUILD A SAFETY FENCE: FENCEPOST

- Educate yourself and your leadership on the myths of human trafficking. Discuss the importance of identifying myths present in anti-human-trafficking efforts.
- Reflect on any ministries, organizations, or anti-human-trafficking efforts your church supports. Can you identify whether the citizen savior mindset is present or any areas where it might tempting to fall into this myth? If so, stop and reassess as a community.

- Discern and fact-check before reposting and sharing stories of modern slavery on social media.

COMMUNITY ASSESSMENT

Sandie Morgan has been training churches and conducting community assessments focused on human trafficking for over twenty years. This section will discuss how your church or organization might undertake such an assessment.

But first, let's consider again the story of the widow whose two sons were saved from the creditors in 2 Kings 4:1-7. Remember that Elisha did not ask his marketing team to develop a video and raise money to pay the woman's debt. That wouldn't have been sustainable, as she would have had new expenses and had to return the following month for more assistance.

When we ask ourselves what is missing in our communities, we naturally want to provide something to alleviate the problems we see. Elisha did not do this. We would be wise to study his example and avoid developing huge mission projects that require ongoing external support and die when the missionary champion retires or church giving falls.

As discussed previously, Elisha engaged in asset-based community development (ABCD), an evidence-based best practice for building communities. ABCD works to support local residents in making their assets visible and to enhance the connection of those assets.[18]

The ABCD Institute has identified three characteristics of an effective implementation of this approach:

1. Local assets are identified.
2. Unconnected assets are connected.
3. Usually, a group or individual acts as the initiating connector.[19]

What assets does a church bring to its community? Most local churches are uniquely positioned in their communities through history, trusted relationships, and established presence. Existing facilities are probably designed for meetings and teaching, perfect for partnering with organizations that have expertise but no meeting location. Churches have people who are already serving in the community as leaders, professionals, volunteers, and active citizens. The Sunday morning platform is one of the church's greatest assets, offering the opportunity to educate and teach prevention. In addition, the church can build empathy in congregations through sermons, Sunday schools, homilies, and small group meetings.

Another asset is the local church's commitment to service and justice. The mandate in Proverbs 31:8 is not optional: "Speak up for those who cannot speak for themselves, for the rights of all who are destitute." This call aligns with the New Testament corollary in James 1:27: "Religion that God our Father accepts as pure and faultless is this: to look after orphans and widows in their distress and to keep oneself from being polluted by the world." The church is to be known in the community by how well it fulfills this mandate to ensure justice for those being crushed. The church fulfills these mandates by being salt and light in the world.

MAKE YOUR CHURCH RELEVANT

LaCinda Bloomfield, Copastor of Champion Church in Yuma, Arizona[20]

The first time I heard the term "human trafficking" was from Sandie Morgan. She was speaking at a conference I was attending. During a break we began talking and I invited her to come to my church and conduct a human trafficking awareness training seminar. In preparation for the seminar our group created ten beautifully packed black-with-pink polka-dotted suitcases, each filled with necessities and all kinds of pretty things for victims of human trafficking. Our gifts were ready to go at any time our local ICE agent called with a human trafficking rescue. We were excited and ready to learn how to combat this ugliest of crimes.

That day Sandie lovingly smacked us all between the eyes when she challenged the paradigm of trying to rescue victims rather than preventing human trafficking in the first place. Sandie said, "You want to prevent human trafficking? I'll tell you exactly how to prevent it. Make your children's church amazing. Make your youth program over the top. Make your church radiant and relevant to the community. Please don't tell me you want to make a difference out there" (she pointed to the doors) "when you are not making a difference in here and now."

REALITY CHECK (BY SANDIE)

I remember the day LaCinda Bloomfield called me. The situation felt urgent because the church's various responses seemed focused on rescue. With my experience, I could see the possible risks. When I met with the leaders and staff that day, I polled the room: "What do you want to do? How are you going to do it?"

Many felt called to do something, and "something" looked like rescue. Someone even had a house they were willing to use as a home for rescued girls. We then turned to the community assessment process.

We asked questions. The Bible says to count the cost (Luke 14:28), so we started there. How much would the home cost? Answers ranged from free to a few hundred dollars for utilities and meals. But we had to do our homework, so we started to discuss laws governing residential programs for children, which included full-time staff around the clock and contingency plans for emergencies, including onsite transportation. There was still excitement in the room for the idea.

Next, we explored where those resources would come from. When we mentioned reallotting ministry salaries, the answer was, "No, we'll have volunteers."

This brought up new questions. Were these volunteers qualified according to child welfare regulations? What risk management expenses would the regulations and the insurance company require? It was quickly becoming clear that counting the cost was a valuable part of the process.

While we were exploring existing church resources, the group told me about an amazing sidewalk dance club ministry they already had in the community. This program used a church van to go to the most vulnerable neighborhoods and connect with kids who had few choices in life. The dance instructor told me about a twelve-year-old who participated in the dance club and was now an active member of the youth group.

We recognized that if we were to open a home for survivors, we would need to use the church van that was currently being used for the dance ministry. We began to see a conflict in reassigning resources. This conflict caused us to pause and ask further questions. Should we wait for a little girl to become a victim in need of rescue? Or should we double our efforts to reach more twelve-year-old girls before they become victims? To open the rescue home, the church would not only need to use its van, but staff salaries would need to be reassigned to staff for the home, causing ministries like the sidewalk dance club to no longer be possible.

Like Elisha, this church identified what they already had in their possession that was connected to their community, fulfilling their mandate to be salt and light. By using what they already had, church leaders saw a twelve-year-old child use her time productively, become part of a loving community, and gain resilience. All of this helped protect this child from eventually being trafficked. In the end, the church people changed their mindset about putting resources toward rescue and instead were able to multiply their resources around prevention.

MAKE YOUR CHURCH COLLABORATIVE

Brian and Kelly Bell, Pastors, Calvary Chapel, Murietta, California

The Lord opened our eyes to the situation of human trafficking about twelve years ago. The more we learned, the more shocked we became and the more we felt compelled to do something about it. We began to educate ourselves through various books and conferences.

As we began our personal journey, we found ourselves desiring to know the best way to counsel and treat survivors. We registered for a four-day training program with Vanguard University's Global Center for Women and Justice called "Hands that Heal." At the end of the program, leaders advised us to contact the human trafficking task force in our county to see how we could help locally.

A few like-minded leaders from church began to meet once a month to pray and seek the Lord on how we should move forward and get involved. We began to volunteer with our task force. Our county is very large, and the task force expressed a need for more awareness to be built in our area, Southern California's Inland Empire. We hosted an awareness event, and although it did create awareness, we wanted to do more. We then asked Sandie Morgan to partner with us, and the annual Justice Matters Conference was created.

We hosted and funded the event, and Sandie was the expert. She helped line up other speakers and created the content for the conference, which became an annual event. We began by hosting it on

Saturdays and welcomed the entire community, as well as local government leaders, business leaders, and local churches. After our fifth year, and after a lot of prayer, we moved the conference from a Saturday event to the Sunday morning platform service so more people would hear the messages. Once a year, on Justice Matters Conference Sunday, we now have workshops to go into more depth on various topics. We invite twenty-five or more relevant community organizations to be exhibitors so people can connect with and support them.

Through all this, we learned the value of collaboration. We learned the importance of prevention, and we are constantly trying to get others to understand the importance of reaching people before they become victims. We learned that one person or organization cannot do everything. We need each other. Competing with each other defeats the purpose and hurts the cause. We learned the importance of what the faith community can do: that everyone can do something and that human trafficking is an issue related to our faith.

WHERE TO START? (BY SANDIE)

Not long ago I was asked by the young pastor of an established church to help them conduct a community assessment focused on combating human trafficking. This was an aging congregation. While the individuals who attended the church had stayed the same, the community around them had changed, becoming less affluent over the years. When I visited, we walked through the church facilities and reviewed the congregant roster. We found only a handful of people under seventy years old. We also identified some absolutely gorgeous Sunday school classrooms. Everything was well-maintained and the young pastor was eager to reach out to his community. As it happened, the church was located two blocks from a middle school.

"What can we do?" they asked. As part of the community assessment, we identified proximity to the middle school, teachers who were willing to volunteer after school, and the children's classrooms with internet access. I recommended they become the church that cares about internet safety for children. The church launched an afterschool program and even expanded to conduct summer trainings as well, using free curriculum from NetSmartz

.org. They began hosting workshops for parents as well as students. This aging congregation, with flip phones and little computer experience, pivoted, learned, and leveraged their collective resources and made change in their community.

This story reflects the ABCD community assessment model:

1. Local assets were identified: classrooms, Wi-Fi, and free resources at NetSmartz.org.
2. Unconnected assets were connected: the church, the middle school, the congregants, and community families.
3. A group or an individual acted as the initiating connector: The young pastor was willing to be creative and as a result initiated change in his church and the community.

Often well-meaning church people ready to start anti-trafficking ministries experience disappointment when faced with the need to focus on assessment and prevention. The path forward is complicated by protocols, policies, and even legal barriers. Instead of learning how to jump on board, some churches complain they are not welcomed to the anti-trafficking table, even going so far as to say they are being persecuted. What is a better way forward?

Go to the place that is darkest in your community and observe the people who are there. How can you build a fence to keep them safe? Can you host a business fair where they can find jobs? Can you develop an afterschool program in a poor district that does not have many resources? There are many options, but it all starts with community assessment. Here is a six-step process I use when guiding churches.

Step one: Look around. As described above, the first step is to start with an assessment of your community, followed by an assessment of your resources. Leave your church building and walk six blocks in every direction. Note any businesses, schools, and other churches (these can be potential partners). Are there kids hanging out by themselves when they should be home? Are there people who are homeless? Are there single moms? Do you see a car in a driveway leaking oil? Maybe that family is one car repair away from not being able to pay their rent. (And, when you get to step two, you may discover someone in your church who is able to fix cars.)

As you map your community, listen to its residents and find out who is already doing something to help—where they are doing it and how effective it is. The Bible actually teaches community assessment when it tells us to consider the cost of a major project: "Suppose one of you wants to build a tower. Won't you first sit down and estimate the cost to see if you have enough money to complete it?" (Luke 14:28).

I once led a training in central California where the attendees were visibly engaged in trauma-informed training and other ways to serve survivors. But they were not enthusiastic about mapping the community and assessing needs or opportunities. Eventually they drew a map of one of the hot spots where people were often being commercially sexually exploited.

They thought they were done at this point. But then I asked, "What is around that area?" I wanted to know everything and get a full picture.

In the midst of the mapping exercise, this group discovered a church located close enough to the area that it could store backpacks and other items for victims, and police officers could pick them up as needed. This team engaged that local church, which became very active. You never know what you're going to find until you seriously perform a thorough assessment.

Step two: Consider people. Church assessment includes a review of people and their expertise, resources, and time, not just facilities and property. The Bible teaches that people are the church, not buildings. In one church where I was offering guidance on community assessment, I asked for an opportunity to meet with church members who might volunteer pro bono professional services. Survivors of labor and sex trafficking, for example, often need dental services—traffickers don't tend to take victims for their annual checkups.

The pastor made the introductions, and the church members who responded turned into long-term trusted volunteers and service providers. A gynecologist committed to adding two pro bono cases a year, and a dentist offered one pro bono appointment per month.

In my experience, churches often show up at local anti-trafficking task force meetings with a list of things they want to do, resources they have, and plans they've made without first finding out what is needed. Anti-human-trafficking programs that are solidly grounded in the community will be ready to engage both the volunteers and those they serve.

Step three: What is the problem? To have a strong community assessment outcome and to build a commitment to collaborate, everyone involved has to agree on the problem to address. Everyone needs to be part of developing the strategy and the plan.

Start with basics. One frequently used tool is called the "problem tree." This is how it works: Draw a tree trunk on posterboard or a whiteboard. This trunk represents the main problem being addressed (human trafficking). Break into small groups, set a timer, and ask each participant to identify what they see as evidence of the problem in their community. Those become the leaves on the tree. Each group then reports to the whole group. Next, the group breaks up again to identify the underlying causes of those problems. Those are the roots.

This exercise is especially helpful in crosscultural environments, whether the neighborhood next door or another country. Empower people in their own community to identify what they see and analyze why those problems exist.

Step four: Innovative solutions. After the problem tree activity, it is time to dream about possible solutions. Nothing is off the table. In this group activity the rules are clear: the facilitator cannot make limits. Everyone has a voice. Everyone brainstorms. We capture every idea. The leader walks around the room to ensure all participants are being heard and considered. Getting input from all individuals is imperative to thoroughly exploring, analyzing, and generating solutions to decide what to do. Facilitators must be accomplished at allowing everyone to have a voice so everyone will own the plan.

Step five: How not to overpromise and underdeliver. Now that the community has identified the problem and brainstormed solutions, we have the difficult task of narrowing down the path forward. For this activity, distribute colored dots or colored marking pens, giving a different color to each participant. Everyone votes for their top three (and only three) choices from the list of ideas, with votes identifiable by color. The next part of this step—coming to consensus on one solution—is challenging, and you may even have a few people drop out of the process. Pray for your participants and ask them to pray for wisdom as you attempt to come to agreement on a project to embark on together. It is important to understand that moving forward with one plan does not eliminate another plan forever; it's just not what we can do right now.

Part of choosing a path forward involves deciding the criteria for any viable project. Start a chart with your top three to five options (based on votes) across the top and columns to compare, contrast, question, and examine what will be needed. Sometimes we have a great idea but it isn't feasible. Perhaps there is no budget or we don't have the expertise. Due diligence is required to carefully assess all project ideas. Remember, just because we can't do it doesn't mean it's a bad idea. But we do need to know if we can sustain it. It is a biblical mandate to count the cost, as Luke 14:28-29 demonstrates: "Suppose one of you wants to build a tower. Won't you first sit down and estimate the cost to see if you have enough money to complete it? For if you lay the foundation and are not able to finish it, everyone who sees it will ridicule you, saying, 'This person began to build and wasn't able to finish.'"

Here's the risk when we do not count the cost. Our church may have a great idea and have enough money to get started, but we can fund it only for a set amount of time. The community, on the other hand, may assume our church is going to continue this program indefinitely. If we don't clearly communicate project limitations to the people we are serving, they may think we promised one thing and delivered something else. This reduces community trust in us. For instance, I know of a church that began a mentoring program for survivors of human trafficking that lasted only one year. After the year was up, the survivors felt abandoned and what little trust they had in Christians was gone.

Once we have agreed on one project by consensus of the group, the team will need to create a budget, identify people and roles, set goals, and make a plan to collect data. Project management models that your church already uses would fit best.

Step six: Did we do what we said we would? The final stage is to monitor and evaluate. This process is ongoing. We develop our evaluation "muscle," and it becomes a best practice. We set goals to know when we are successful, and we evaluate. As we evaluate, we may discover gaps we overlooked, and this will help us improve or build new collaborations. Whether we are working with survivors of trafficking or with vulnerable communities trying to prevent it, growing our networks and our collaborative partnerships can increase our success and sustainability. We can access more programs and tackle more problems if we partner in our communities.

One of the things a church or organization has to decide is how it fits in its community. This will be addressed further in chapter six, but for now we can note that it is a critical aspect of how the church shows up. How did Jesus approach people? He looked at their need before he offered anything. What is the need in your community? What resources do you have? What expertise do you bring? Don't volunteer for something you can't sustain. Volunteer for what you can sustain and then be faithful.

SHOW UP AND DON'T GO IT ALONE

The church is the hope of the world because we are empowered by the Holy Spirit. Victory is already ours in Christ's resurrection. Individuals caught in exploitation don't have hope, but they can observe our hope rooted deeply in the love and truth of Jesus Christ. We keep showing up in order to spread transformational love and make disciples. Matthew 28:19 reminds us that as we are going—walking with people in our community, like Jesus did—we are making disciples. If we don't show up, who will they walk with?

Our mandate is to be a voice for those who have no voice and ensure justice for those being crushed (Proverbs 31:8). When we design programs to fight human trafficking, we have to remember that we can't do it alone. If we try, we will burn out, and then a lot of other people suffer. It is not ethical to fight human trafficking alone; we as individuals and churches always have to be part of a team. We were created to be the body of Christ, and we need our members to do this well.

BUILD A SAFETY FENCE: FENCEPOSTS

- As a church, become familiar with the asset-based community development (ABCD) model.
  - Identify the assets in your church.
  - Identify where unconnected assets in your church and community can be connected.
  - Identify the group or individual who has the capacity to initiate greater connection with church and community.
- Execute your own six-step assessment process (find a qualified facilitator if needed).
  - Begin by mapping your own community.
  - Review your congregational body and look at members' expertise, resources, and available time in order to understand how they can be an asset to your church's response to human trafficking.
  - With a facilitator, identify the problems in your community by doing the problem tree activity.
  - Generate solutions to the problem you discovered.
  - Analyze the viability of your chosen solution and set realistic goals.
  - Monitor and evaluate the goals you set on a regular schedule.
- Throughout this process, do not go it alone. Work diligently to find collaborators in this work.

4

PROTECTION

IDENTIFY AND REPORT

The best defense against modern-day slavery is a vigilant public. Be a nosy neighbor.

KEVIN BALES

PROTECTION FOCUSES ON empowering survivors of human trafficking with a renewed sense of personal dignity. It involves recovering, restoring, and reintegrating these survivors into society. But the first step is identifying those individuals who may be in bondage. Modern slavery and human trafficking are happening right under our noses, affecting people we encounter as we go through our days without giving them a second thought. Below is a list of common places and situations where slavery has been documented in the United States, as well as signs that someone may be a human trafficking victim. Read through the list, keeping in mind the people around your town and church who might work in these types of environments. Consider creating resources for your church and disseminate them to raise awareness and boost human trafficking literacy within your community.

WHERE TO LOOK FOR AND IDENTIFY SLAVERY

Here are some common places and situations where slavery has been known to flourish:

- Housecleaning services
- Landscape and gardening businesses
- Households in which domestic home workers are present
- Large-scale agriculture operations
- Construction sites
- Casinos
- Garment factories
- Hotels (especially in housekeeping departments)
- Nail salons
- Migrant or transitional communities
- Zones known for commercial sexual exploitation
- Strip clubs
- Massage parlors
- Domestic violence situations

WHAT TO LOOK FOR TO IDENTIFY HUMAN TRAFFICKING VICTIMS

The following are signs that someone may be a human trafficking victim. Many of these signs on their own are enough to raise concern and a reason to call the National Human Trafficking Hotline or local law enforcement. But more often it is a constellation of these signals that provides evidence that a person is trapped in modern slavery. When you suspect human trafficking, it is important to never put yourself, volunteers, or the victim in danger. Call the hotline number: 888-373-7888. In the international community, use the United Nations or local government websites to find information on how to report your concerns.

Individuals may be victims of human trafficking if they

- Are not free to come and go as they wish
- Are not free to change employers

- Are afraid to discuss themselves in the presence of others
- Do not control their earnings
- Are unpaid or paid very little
- Have few or no personal possessions
- Are not in control of their own money or have no financial records or bank account
- Are not in control of their own identification documents
- Are not allowed or able to speak for themselves (e.g., a third party insists on being present or interpreting)
- Have an attorney they do not seem to know or did not agree to receive representation services from
- Work excessively long or unusual hours
- Are not allowed breaks or suffer under unusual restrictions at work
- Owe a large or increasing debt and are unable to pay it off
- Were recruited through false promises concerning the nature and conditions of their work
- Are living or working in a location with high security measures (e.g., opaque or boarded-up windows, bars on windows, barbed wire, security cameras)
- Exhibit unusual fearful, anxious, depressed, submissive, tense, nervous, or paranoid behavior
- React with unusually fearful or anxious behavior at any reference to law enforcement
- Avoid eye contact
- Exhibit a flat affect (e.g., do not display emotion, seem "blank" or unresponsive)
- Exhibit unexplained injuries or signs of prolonged or untreated illness or disease
- Appear malnourished

- Are under eighteen years of age and are providing commercial sex acts
- Are in the commercial sex industry and have a pimp or manager
- Show signs of physical or sexual abuse, physical restraint, confinement, or torture
- Have been "branded" by a trafficker (e.g., a tattoo of the trafficker's name)
- Claim to be "just visiting" and are unable to clarify where they are
- Exhibit a lack of knowledge of whereabouts or do not know what city they are in
- Exhibit a loss of a sense of time
- Have numerous inconsistencies in their story

Young people might be caught in sex trafficking or are actively being recruited if they

- Display a significant change in behavior, including increased time online or on screens or associating with a new group of friends
- Avoid answering questions or let others speak for them
- Appear frightened, resistant, or belligerent to law enforcement
- Lie about their age and identity
- Look to others before answering questions
- Do not ask for help or resist offers to get out of the situation (do not self-identify as a victim)
- Seem coached in talking to law enforcement
- Use trafficking-related terms like *trick*, *the life*, or *the game*
- Are preoccupied with "getting money" (e.g., displaying photos of cash)
- Have unexplained absences from school for a period of time
- Are unable to attend school on a regular basis
- Repeatedly run away from home
- Make references to frequent travel to other cities
- Exhibit bruises or other physical trauma, withdrawn behavior, depression, or fear

- Lack control over their schedule or identification documents
- Are hungry or malnourished and dress inappropriately for weather conditions or surroundings
- Show signs of drug addiction[1]

There are many documented cases of labor and sex trafficking each year, with some dramatic rescues and busts. A more subtle form of slavery found in our backyards is the enslavement of domestic help. Often working up to sixteen hours a day, victims of domestic servitude make up the second-highest form of slavery in the United States. Most are foreigners and work under threats of violence. Afraid to run away, they often work in isolation due to a language barrier or lack of interaction with others. Domestic slaves live quietly in fear—fear of deportation, fear of beatings, fear of the well-being of other family members, or fear of humiliation. These fears keep domestic slaves hidden and submissive.

A CASE STUDY

Shyima was one of twelve children, originally from Egypt, when she was sold to another Egyptian family at eight years old. This family eventually moved to the United States and settled in Irvine, California. Shyima slept on a mattress on the floor of the garage and was not allowed to go to school. She spent each day cooking and cleaning and caring for the family's five children from morning to night. Her captors told her she would never see her family again if she tried to flee or if she told anyone about her situation. They also told her law enforcement would beat her and take her to jail. So rather than trusting the police for help, she feared them. For two years Shyima lived as a domestic slave in the United States, rarely stepping outside the door of the house where she worked. Shyima was rescued because a neighbor noticed a child who didn't go to school and law enforcement was asked to do a welfare check.

Years later when Shyima was an adult she was interviewed for a training video to teach others what domestic slavery might look like. She said not knowing the language, fear of law enforcement, and physical and psychological threats were what kept her from running away.

Many stories have been uncovered about domestic slaves eventually finding freedom. Some risk it all and run, but many are discovered and assisted because of the action of a diligent public, because someone in the community knew what to look for, identified a possible victim of human trafficking, and reported it.

Knowing how to identify the red flags of human trafficking can change your community. Tracy, a woman living in a comfortable suburb, once asked the woman who cleaned her house how she immigrated to the United States. Tracy learned that Elise originally came to the United States on a work visa to work in a restaurant. When she began, the manager took her documents and told her she would get them back after she had worked there for six years.

Tracy voiced her concerns and asked many more questions, but Elise told her it had worked out okay for her and her husband; they worked at the restaurant for six years and were both able to become legal citizens. "But I do fear for the others still there," Elise said. "The manager has become more strict and it is not a good place to work."

Tracy asked Elise if she would consider telling the police about what the manager was doing. Tracy explained that what was happening is illegal under the Trafficking Victims Protection Act and her friends would be able to get some help. Elise told Tracy she did not trust police. Knowing she would not be able to convince Elise to report the situation, Tracy contacted her local human trafficking task force, which put her in touch with law enforcement. A few months later, Tracy followed up to see how the case was coming. "Let's just say it was a very good tip," said the officer. He could not tell her much more than that, but Tracy now understood that she could do something—that sometimes a small act such a phone call tip changes a person's situation and life.

Tracy's story illustrates not just the importance of being educated and able to identify human trafficking, it also illustrates the importance of reporting. Regular citizens are not trained in law enforcement and should never interject themselves into suspected cases of human trafficking. This might result in disruption of an ongoing investigation by police, harm to yourself, or harm to the victim. Traffickers are criminals, and they are dangerous. Always report and educate your communities on how to report.

BUILD A SAFETY FENCE: FENCEPOSTS

- Create sermons, lessons, and studies around identifying vulnerabilities and victims of human trafficking.
- Make reporting policies clear for your leadership, staff, congregation, and organization.
- Ask questions of the people around you and build relationships.
- Explore as a church how you can be eyes and ears for your community.
- Post the National Human Trafficking Hotline number around your church and ensure everyone in your community is aware of it: 888-373-7888.

VICTIMS' NEEDS AND TRAUMA SIGNS

"One of my first memories was when my sister was hospitalized. She was sixteen years old and I was only nine," says Louise, a survivor of human trafficking. "She told the hospital psychiatrist that my dad raped her. Nothing happened. The hospital did nothing. She was released back with our family. My dad was involved in a cult in Laguna Beach, California. A guy by the name of Wolf was the leader. He sexually trafficked kids both within the adults of the cult as well as sold them outside the group for profit."

Louise spent many years being trafficked and abused before she was able to escape that life, and now she helps others as a therapist. But her journey as a survivor in the church has not been an easy one. The stories of survivors' experiences can challenge and convict leaders as we repent and move to more spiritually healthy responses.

LOUISE, A SURVIVOR, SHARES HER STORY

The stories survivors of human trafficking share are unique. It is critical that the church handle these stories and victims with respect and dignity. It is not important, or even appropriate, for the church to know all the graphic details of this crime. Rather, what is essential is that leaders have tools to care for survivors.

Starting at eighteen years old, I shared my experience about once a year with someone in the church who I thought was safe. Each time I shared my story, the same thing happened. Nothing. Now, at age seventy and having been a therapist for most of my adult life, I know not to take it personally, but it does not mean it does not or did not hurt. I think people do not know what to say and so they say nothing and later avoid the subject altogether. They might be people who I know still love me, but they simply don't know what to do or say, so they avoid it.

At one point I felt close to our pastor. My husband and I felt like he and his wife, who was also a therapist, were good friends. I shared with him what happened to me as a child. I could tell by the look on his face he did not know what to do with the information. At the end of our awkward conversation he said he would get back to me to discuss further.

He never did.

This particular situation when I disclosed my story was more painful than others. I didn't need his counseling services. I didn't need answers. I shared to be understood by someone who I viewed as a spiritual mentor. He was my spiritual leader, and his lack of follow-up was one of the more disorienting and triggering encounters of my adult life. I think with a little information and humility, church leaders—and really anybody—can do a better job responding to trafficking and trauma victims.

As a Christian, a trafficking survivor, and a therapist, I wish pastors and church leaders knew three simple things they could do: Listen. Ask questions. Follow up.

Church leaders and pastors do not have to have all the answers, but they do need to know how to listen and how to ask empathic and trauma-informed questions. Most importantly, they need to get back in touch with the person. Following up might look like a phone call or email acknowledging the conversation. It may be referring the individual to a counselor they can contact if they don't already have one. Or it could simply be checking in to see how they are feeling after sharing something so vulnerable.

When pastors and church leaders never acknowledge the pain, this causes already victimized people to feel dismissed, abandoned, and shamed. By listening well and following up with the person, a church leader can avoid double abuse. If people do not respond appropriately, this can cause additional harm and abuse to the survivor.

As Louise's story illustrates, it's important for churches and leaders to explore what they are doing (or not doing) to prepare themselves, staff, and volunteers to deal with those who come to them with stories of past trauma. In addition, when dealing with victims of human trafficking and exploitation, language matters. If you have been doing human trafficking work, you are familiar with the word "rescue" in regard to individuals being removed from trafficking situations. In these situations, a better word to use is "recovery." Those coming out of trafficking situations have a long road to healing, and the word "rescue" does not convey the long-term effects of trauma on their lives.

The US Department of Health and Human Service explains, "The emotional effects of trauma can be persistent and devastating. Victims of human trafficking may suffer from anxiety, panic disorder, major depression, substance abuse, and eating disorders as well as a combination of these. For some victims, the trauma induced by someone they once trusted results in pervasive mistrust of others and their motives. This impact of trauma can make the job of first responders and those trying to help victims difficult at best."[2]

As the church, we are uniquely positioned to be first responders. Many individuals in our church pews and organizations carry unspoken trauma, even if not from human trafficking. The church is never expected to take the place of a professional therapist, social worker, or psychologist, but when the church is trauma-informed, we can assist survivors of trauma by referring and reporting well.

THE JOURNEY TO HEALING

Simone Halpin, Executive Director of Naomi's House

Healing from sexual trauma does not happen overnight. It takes time. Sometimes a long time. And healing is individual to each victim, not a one-size-fits-all journey. What I have learned while working with dozens of victims from sex trafficking is that their trauma keeps them locked in the past, traumatizing them over and over. What a victim needs is a comprehensive healing pathway that allows to them to therapeutically, spiritually, and practically address their trauma so they can live in the present and dream about their future.

Imagine sitting at the kitchen table with your dad as he heats milk and adds hot cocoa mix while a piece of toast pops up. He stops, spreads a little butter on the toast, sprinkles it with cinnamon, and cuts it diagonally. He brings two cups of steaming hot chocolate and the toast to the table. Imagine you have just had a terrible nightmare. But now you are awake and being reminded you are safe and loved. Later in life, whenever you smell hot chocolate, this vivid memory is what comes to mind.

Our minds are huge filing cabinets full of memories that we access as best we can when we need information from our past. In fact, often we do not go looking for our memories; they simply pop up. You may not remember what caused the terrible nightmare, yet it is cemented in your memories and resolves when the smell of hot chocolate fills the air. But what if you had awakened from the nightmare and it only turned worse? What if every time you smelled the aroma of hot chocolate, you were filled with fear and dread instead?

What if a victim of human trafficking was awakened in the middle of the night and given hot chocolate? And what if you did not know that was a routine part of his trafficking experience when you invited him to your church program? You are attempting to be warm and welcoming, and when the survivor insists he does not want any hot chocolate, you playfully insist he must drink some. You may be confused because you did not get the reaction you were expecting. Trauma causes individuals to react in many ways, including shutting down when feeling threatened.

A church leader needs to plan for the safety of those being served as well as those serving. Being trauma-informed means you are able to anticipate how someone might respond to a trigger from a previous traumatic experience. It means you put your personal preferences and expectations aside. It also means you don't dig and ask the same questions repeatedly. You give them space.

Here's an example from a visit with a multidisciplinary team that met to determine a good housing placement for an adolescent survivor. A family member had made arrangements for housing placement with a Christian ministry. This facility was not usually an option for the team, but they agreed to try it in this case, and a call was made on speakerphone so the team could participate in the initial intake. The well-intentioned program director on the other end was glad to explain that this was a new ministry for trafficking victims and immediately asked, "How were you sex-trafficked?" The girl was silent, so the program director asked again, but the girl remained quiet. When she asked again, more loudly, the girl sheepishly asked the team if she could please pick up the phone and get off speakerphone. This intake process was not trauma-informed.

In cases of child abuse, it is important not to ask children and youth to tell their story over and over again. The same is true with trafficking victims. Trauma leaves deep emotional and psychological scars that continue to cause pain when victims remember and verbalize their traumatic experiences. A major study by the Centers for Disease Control and Kaiser Permanente, the ACE Study of adverse childhood experiences, has shown how childhood experiences predict our future health, including mental, behavioral, and physical health.[3] Adverse childhood experiences even affect how opportunity works in our life. In a trauma-informed approach, studies like these can guide how we help prevent the most vulnerable from becoming victims of human trafficking and how we support victims and intervene on their behalf.

Being trauma-informed means we think before we speak and are careful how we ask about survivors' stories. We do not need details in order to feed them and take care of them. They decide when and if they want to tell their story. For those with an interest in serving victims of trauma, including sexual trauma, resources providing best practices include a guide from the US Department of Health and Human Services as well as the book *Understanding Sexual Abuse* by Tim Hein.[4]

Imagine being a survivor with a horrific story in your past and a marvelous story of recovery as well. In counseling you have been encouraged to leave the past behind and learn new patterns of thinking, living, and being. Counselors often work with their patients to literally develop new neurological pathways, and the Bible supports the science. Romans 12:2 says, "Be transformed by the renewing of your mind," and Philippians 4:8 offers guidance on thinking about things that are true and have virtue. But

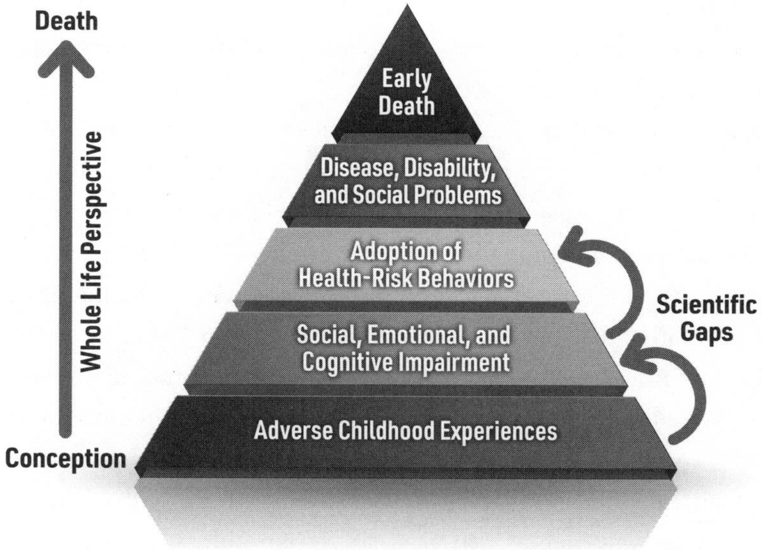

Figure 2. Adverse childhood experiences pyramid

as a survivor, you have been asked to tell your story again and again during occasions such as court appearances, awareness events, and fundraisers. Is that best for you?

One survivor we know has explained, "Sometimes people don't understand that when I tell my story, I actually dissociate." There is a cost to this narrative. Dissociation is a protective mechanism, and part of being trauma-informed is understanding this cost.

There are a few basic tips church leaders can follow to be trauma-informed. If someone cannot make eye contact and talks about their experiences while looking off into a corner, they may be dissociating. What should we do in this situation? We need to recognize that this person cannot handle the conversation now and we may not be qualified to help them, so we need to find referral services. We do not need to have all the details about a survivor's story. Unfortunately, churches often do want every detail, and this tendency is salacious and harmful.

A better practice is to follow the lead of male police officers. They are trained that when they encounter a child who has been sexually abused or exploited, they get the child to a safe space and invite a female officer or someone with trauma-informed social work training to be present before anyone asks questions.

We should note here the distinction between post-traumatic stress disorder (PTSD) and generalized trauma. A traumatic event is time-based, while PTSD is a longer-term condition where one continues to have flashbacks and re-experience the traumatic event. PTSD can be part of the trauma response of a person coming out of a human trafficking situation, but that individual can also experience basic trauma. According to the Substance Abuse and Mental Health Services Administration (SAMHSA), trauma results from "an event, series of events, or set of circumstances that is experienced by an individual as physically or emotionally harmful or life threatening and that has lasting adverse effects on the individual's functioning and mental, physical, social, emotional, or spiritual well-being."[5] Trauma arises not only from physical or psychological abuse; the triggering event can be anything that causes a lasting effect on that person's sense of well-being. In addition, victims remember the feelings they felt during the traumatic experience much more readily than they do the specific circumstances.

Sometimes it is difficult for people working with survivors—service providers, law enforcement officers, teachers, university professors, or pastors—to identify trauma. Trauma can look like difficulty following through on commitments, avoiding meetings, self-isolating, engaging in interpersonal conflict, being easily agitated, and becoming aggressive. Survivors often demonstrate lack of trust and can even feel that everybody is against them in a kind of a conspiracy mentality. Often they end up in other abusive relationships. Sometimes they start abusing substances in order to escape.

Being trauma-informed means your organization or church has a framework to understand that the people you serve may be victims of trauma in the past. Being trauma-informed gives your people a grounding and an understanding of the impact of trauma on individuals. When we see any evidence of triggering due to trauma, we extend grace and understanding in the face of frustrating and confusing behavior.

Another quality of being trauma-informed is that we do not excuse bad behavior, but we do use a strengths-based service delivery approach, such as building on resilience and asset development. Research has demonstrated that responding to trauma in a way that creates emotional safety for both the provider and the survivor creates opportunities for survivors to rebuild a sense of control and empowerment.[6]

For instance, say an individual arrives at our small group at church and that person is combative, stands off to the side, and refuses to engage with other people. Do we respond by saying, "You are disruptive and have been given many chances. You can't come anymore"? Not if we are trauma-informed and looking for ways to give that individual a sense of control and empowerment. A trauma-informed response might sound like, "I understand that you do not want to join the group right now. Would you like to sit over here on the side?" We allow that person to make a choice and experience a sense of agency.

For churches and organizations that want to learn more, SAMHSA discusses the four Rs of a program or system that is trauma-informed:

- *Realizes* the widespread impact of trauma and the potential paths for recovery.
- *Recognizes* the symptoms of trauma in clients and their families.
- *Responds* by fully integrating trauma-informed practices in policies and guidelines of ministries.
- Avoids *retraumatization*. That is our goal. We do not want to traumatize people any further.[7]

Public health agencies have identified the prevalence of trauma in our nation. According to their research, 98 percent of female offenders in our social service system have had an experience with trauma, most often interpersonal and domestic violence. Ninety-six percent of adolescent psychiatric inpatients have histories of exposure to trauma. Ninety-three percent of homeless mothers have a lifetime history of interpersonal trauma. And in our juvenile justice system, 90 percent of youth have had multiple traumas from an early age, while 75 percent of adults with substance abuse disorder have histories of trauma.[8]

In a trauma-informed system, we have to recognize and promote resilience and healing. Churches and organizations should ask, “Do we have a trauma-informed training program? Do we have trauma-informed policies? What are the guidelines for our church or organization?” In one conversation we had with a nonprofit that does outreach in the community, the volunteers expressed disappointment that clients were not responding in the way they were expecting. Their conclusion was that the clients were not grateful. Yet doing this kind of work and being trauma-informed reminds us that it is not about us. What these volunteers needed was trauma-informed training.

When we are not trauma-informed, we may approach care from the perspective of repair, when what we really need to do is promote the growth of missing connections, or regeneration. Otherwise it’s as if we are trying to hang a picture on a wall that does not exist. We now have powerful tools to take pictures of brain structures, including the neuronal pathways that carry signals from the amygdala to different parts of the brain. We all experience fear and know the feeling of wanting to run or of getting ready to fight. That’s the fight-or-flight response. A third fear response is to freeze. As we mature, the analytical part of our brain in the prefrontal cortex begins to learn that we do not need to run at every sudden noise. We learn to get more information before we panic. However, for a child who has lived in chronic trauma, the pathways to the automatic responses of fight, flight, or freeze are well-worn avenues, and the pathways to more analytical reasoning are not well-developed. When we look at images of a healthy brain and the brain of someone experiencing abuse or chronic stress, we can see the difference: the stressed individual has fewer connections. Trauma is not just psychological and emotional. It is physiological.

This means the term “rehabilitation” may misrepresent the work ahead for a victim of complex trauma, especially someone with a history of trauma as a child. The lack of connection between the amygdala (the brain structure that senses fear) and the prefrontal cortex (the thinking brain) makes it difficult for the victim to think clearly. Instead they go straight to the survival response of fight or flight. In normal child development, attachment forms as part of the parent-child relationship in the early years. The child learns to trust that the caregiver will respond to their cries, and this trust creates attachment. This enables other developmental processes to occur.

Years later, a ninety-day program will not be able to fill in the physical structures that are missing in the brain of a victim of complex trauma. Entire pathways are missing in this person's brain, pathways associated with self-regulation, risk management, and logic. Instead, the amygdala's fear response takes predominance. It can hijack the brain and send out a rush of hormones even in response to a memory and not something actually happening. Its only role is to keep the person safe, so it activates the brain to fight or flee—nothing else. The good news is that the brain is plastic and can be trained, allowing new pathways to develop. God designed us for healing, but it is a long-term process for victims of complex trauma.

TRAUMA-INFORMED DECISIONS

When we make a commitment to be trauma-informed as a community, we need to understand that our compassion is grounded in Christ's love, and that love does not give up. At the same time, we want this trauma-informed community not to blame the victims for things they cannot change. A trauma-informed capacity scale tool is available from the University of Florida[9] as well as the American Institute for Research[10] to help you evaluate and assess gaps in your organization. The development of these tools was funded by your tax dollars, so use the resources you have paid for.

Other skills your team will need to develop include those associated with resilience. Telling someone they are okay, they are smart, and they are beautiful is kind, but it is not enough. Learn to emphasize skills that promote mastery, relationship, and personal control while decreasing emotional reactivity. Equip your church to do these things. It takes practice, but it will bring big dividends.

We all desire to rescue and set people free, yet we must honor the way God designed human beings. Individuals who have experienced trauma may deny being victims. They might be cavalier and insist they are in "the life" because they want to be. They may be resistant to any kind of assistance from you. But when and if they reach the point of contemplation (more on this below) and start to consider what has happened to them, they may acknowledge it is not what they really wanted to do.

The reality is that when we serve survivors well, they will keep coming back. They will know they are loved with agape love, not a passing passion that wanes. Christian leaders can draw on two principles. First, research confirms that the stages of change model (see figure 3) is a relevant framework for working with victims of human trafficking and any other form of trauma. These victims have learned how to survive and may not quickly adapt to their new status of being free.[11] The second principle is that as Christians we never give up. Like the disciples, we may tire of giving someone one more chance. But when Peter asked how many times to

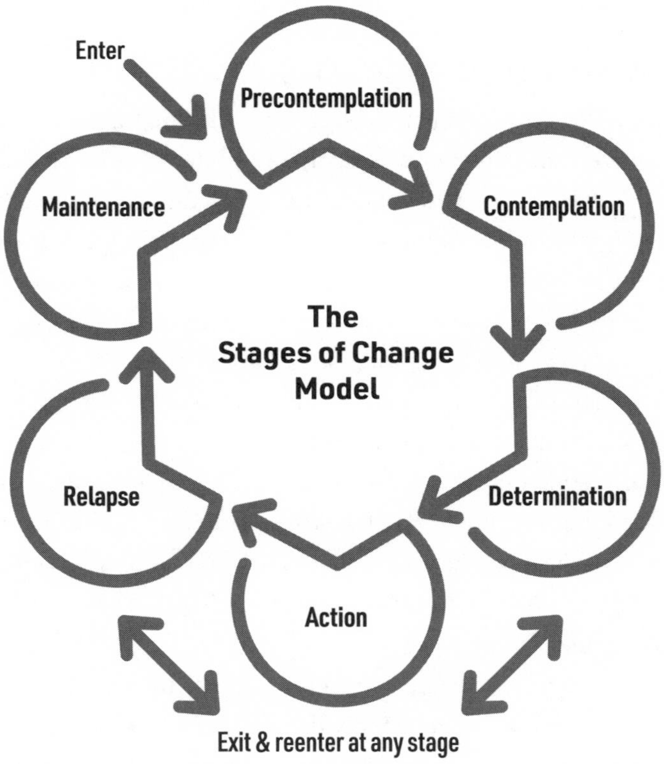

Figure 3. Stages of change model

forgive, suggesting seven times, Jesus answered, "I do not say to you seven times, but seventy times seven" (Matthew 18:21-22 RSV).

The diagram in figure 3 shows the process as a cycle that begins with no awareness that change is possible or needed. Then one begins to consider what it would take to make a change. Determination builds as the hope for change results in a plan of action. Everyone celebrates the victory. The individual is free. Yet there is often a relapse and the cycle starts over. People can enter and exit at any stage until finally they stay in the maintenance lane. This is also a common pattern seen with domestic violence victims; they leave their abusers and return several times before becoming totally free.

Nehemiah did not have a party when the captives returned to Jerusalem. He wept (Nehemiah 1:4). He knew that without a full restoration, the cycle of pillaging would begin again with new marauders and his people would need rescuing again. He developed a strategy to rebuild the walls and build new gates. His strategy required the newly freed slaves to do their part, the hard work of using their old broken rubble to build. It also included outside help to provide for the new gates.

BUILD A SAFETY FENCE: FENCEPOSTS

- Implement mandatory trauma-informed training for all volunteers, ministers, and leaders.
- Learn to use skills that promote mastery, relationship, and personal control while decreasing emotional reactivity. Equip your church to do these things.
- Analyze programs in your church or organization and explore ways your community can assist and be part of someone's ongoing story of recovery and restoration.

PROTECTING CHILDREN

Around the world, everyone agrees that children should be protected from violence, sexual abuse, crime, and forced labor. But what everyone agrees on and the reality of what many children face can be very different. When it comes to protecting children, it is helpful to understand the difference between the role of warning and the roles of protection and practice. Let's take dental decay as an example. We can warn children that if they eat lollipops, they will get cavities in their teeth. We can even create a red flag poster showing the foods that cause the most cavities.

However, we know small children do not have the developmental ability to understand the connection between sugar and a toothache. So we follow a simple public health model: we predict what will cause harm, we develop a strategy to protect from that harm, and we practice that strategy until it becomes a habit.

- Step one: Predict that eating lollipops contributes to tooth decay.
- Step two: Protect by brushing your teeth regularly.
- Step three: Practice by teaching children to protect their own teeth before they understand why.

Brushing your teeth is good, and through the science of medicine we have learned that keeping enamel strong is also important. Following this model, the health community now predicts that weakened enamel increases the risk of dental decay, so cities add fluoride to water and toothpaste manufacturers add ingredients designed to strengthen enamel as well.

The same is true in protecting children from commercial sexual exploitation and forced labor. Effective prevention includes protecting children and youth from recruitment and exploitation by implementing the model of predict, protect, and practice.

The first step is to predict possible avenues for predators to approach a child. Are they volunteers in a club or sports activity? Are they approaching children online through games or social media by pretending to be a friend and then grooming them for exploitation?

Once risks have been identified, it's time to develop a plan to protect children or youth before they are abused or exploited. Teaching children healthy boundaries for their own bodies is an important aspect of protection. Most child sexual abuse is by a person known to the child, not a stranger. In our contemporary community, online predators present themselves as friends to the child. "Stranger danger" prevention models are therefore not very effective, because predators are either already familiar to their victims or make themselves so. Resources for teaching online safety are available for free at NetSmartz.org, a part of the National Center for Missing and Exploited Children.

However, just as a child must be taught to brush her teeth to prevent cavities, so protection from exploitation must be practiced regularly. Schools are adding internet citizenship to their curricula to include internet safety guidelines. Much like a parent teaches a child to "look both ways" when crossing the street, now a parent must teach a child to be sure the person they are talking to is who they say they are.

Polaris Project, a leading US-based organization in human trafficking awareness and prevention, explains how children are typically lured into trafficking situations so communities can be aware and know how to protect them:

> What most people think they know about child sex trafficking generally involves stories—young girls and boys being kidnapped by strangers, forced into windowless vans, then driven to another city or state where they are kept drugged and chained in a brothel.
>
> While situations like these do exist, they are more of an exception than the rule. A study analyzing press releases and online media reports from over a nine-year period found that fewer than 10 percent of cases involved kidnapping. The rest were far more complicated, far less "Hollywood." The danger of these misconceptions is that while we are on high alert for windowless vans and teaching our children about stranger danger, we may well be missing out on what is really going on. There is still a tremendous amount to learn about human trafficking in the United States and far more data and research is needed. But what we do know is a great deal about how victims—particularly young people—are lured into trafficking situations. The information below summarizes some of the best available research about how trafficking actually happens, so you can help to keep your families and communities safe.
>
> Traffickers tend to prey on people who are economically or socially vulnerable such as youth who are living in poverty, or on the streets, or experience physical or sexual abuse, or addiction. They pose as a friend, offering meals, gifts, or just a sympathetic ear. In some cases, traffickers may use another young person to befriend and recruit their victims. This recruitment can happen in public places such as malls or sporting events, as well as online,

through social media sites, or through false advertisements or promises about job opportunities that might appeal to young people, such as modeling or acting. Although runaway and homeless youth are particularly vulnerable, there are also several examples of victims who were groomed and recruited while living at home and even attending school.

Using these methods, over time the trafficker is no longer a stranger, but someone the victim knows and even trusts. With this trust in place, traffickers don't need to kidnap their victims. They can convince them to show up willingly. This perceived choice in the beginning often results in feelings of shame, guilt, or self-blame for victims and survivors who later try to leave their traffickers.

It is also not uncommon for parents and family members to sell children for sex in exchange for money, drugs, or something of value. In these situations, the trafficker is already someone with proximity to the victim and knows enough about the victim to even isolate and manipulate them.

Being aware of and focusing on the ways in which traffickers gradually lure their victims is critical in recognizing and even preventing situations of sex trafficking.[12]

PROTECTING THE INSTITUTIONALIZED CHILD

Both locally and globally, the best practice for protecting children is ensuring they remain in a family setting. The original biological family unit is the most beneficial for the safety, growth, and general well-being of children. When this is not possible, finding a solution that is appropriate and culturally sensitive and still keeps a child in a family caregiving setting may be a good alternative. The removal of a child from the family should be considered only as a last resort. As the Department of State reports, "Studies have found that both private and government-run residential institutions for children, or places such as orphanages and psychiatric wards that do not offer a family-based setting, cannot replicate the emotional companionship and attention found in family environments that are prerequisites to healthy cognitive development."[13]

There are about eight million institutionalized children worldwide, and these children are particularly vulnerable to human trafficking. The physical and psychological effects of staying in residential institutions, combined with societal isolation and often subpar regulatory oversight by governments, put these children at high risk. Because they are not raised in a family-of-origin environment, institutionalized children do not have the same kind of resilience other children do and typically struggle academically. This vulnerability is seen globally in orphanages and also domestically in foster youth. Foster programs are designed to remove a child from a dangerous environment, but when healthy home placements are not available, group homes become the last resort. Efforts to curb this challenging reality are critical to reducing the vulnerability of children and youth.

In orphanages around the world, children are often donor-supported, and they are trained by the orphanages to be nice to any adult who comes to visit. They are often told to be polite and say thank you and are even urged to give hugs. This seemingly simple "trained for niceness" attribute can make these children even more vulnerable to traffickers. This is not the only problem with the traditional orphanage model of caring for children. Rampant fraud has also been documented in orphanage systems around the world.

We believe the best way for churches to avoid falling victim to orphanage fraud is to establish policies to support family-based-care organizations and strategies rather than traditional orphanages. In fact, many missions organizations have moved away from institutionalized models and now are supporting family-based care.

If your church desires to protect vulnerable children from trafficking, become a church that both supports families' needs and fosters children. We know that up to 90 percent of children in institutions have at least one living family member, often even a living parent. Finding ways to support a parent so he or she can adequately care for the child is best for the child and most sustainable long-term for the community. However, fostering is also an excellent way to protect vulnerable children. While there is no substitute for a family setting for the growth and safety of a child, when a child is in danger because of abuse, sexual abuse, or neglect, the local church community can be part of the safety net offering that healthy family setting.

One concern we would like to bring to the attention of the church in its desire to protect children is "voluntourism," or volunteer tourism. This is when individuals visit a country for only a short period to volunteer with an orphanage or other institution. While these volunteers may think their money is going toward helping the children, it often ends up in the pockets of orphanage owners and directors. Voluntourism also can lead to the proliferation of child finders—people who go into nearby impoverished villages and incentivize parents to release their children to these institutions. This is a perfect example of "when helping hurts,"[14] and it is a serious issue the church needs to address. As Christians, our heart for orphans in the world is true and sincere and we have a biblical mandate to care for them. But this world is full of darkness, and we need to be wise as serpents and innocent as doves now more than ever when protecting vulnerable children.

All too often ill-managed institutions are themselves guilty of organizing or facilitating the trafficking of resident children. Before donating to an organization that claims it cares for children, ensure it is legitimate by informing yourself of its credentials, policies, and ultimately what's really happening there.

As a result of a lack of family environment, children who leave or age out of institutions experience increased vulnerability because they are starved for attention, lack a social support network, do not have social maturities such as trust appropriateness, and overall fall short in managing risk. Supporting organizations that provide services to youth transitioning out of the foster program and otherwise supporting mentorship for adolescents and young adults is some of the most powerful and long-term sustaining work we can do to prevent young people from being trafficked or exploited. This is encouraging news, as this is a practical and tangible thing people in every church can do in the fight against human trafficking in their community and beyond.

CONSEQUENCES OF INSTITUTIONAL LIVING

***Leonie Webster, Health-Care Professional*[15]**

I first went to Honduras in 2003, mainly for a short-term mission trip to go and observe clinical need within the remit of midwifery and obstetrics. I was thrown into the arena of orphaned and vulnerable children because the clinic I worked in was next door to an orphanage, a residential facility. I quickly became aware of the huge needs of legally orphaned and vulnerable children at high social risk, especially in a country with high conflict and political instability.

While there, I was invited to partner with some international missionaries who were looking after seventeen children in a very small, beautiful Christian orphanage. It was very difficult to see the realities of early institutional living for children who were legally abandoned or orphaned.

Consequences of institutional living largely depend on the age of entry and how long the child remains in the residential facility. I saw a catalog of symptoms and behaviors among the children: psychosocial relationship problems, learning delays, cognitive development delays, disturbances and delays in physical growth, speech, and social development, low emotional intelligence, and inappropriate or absent boundaries. Many of these behaviors just seemed normal among the children. In addition, I witnessed many incidences of anxiety, withdrawal, and depression. It was apparent very quickly that all was not well within the walls of this Christian residential facility.

I want to make it clear that all of this was well-intentioned and basic life needs were being met. There was food, there was a place to lay your head, there was physical safety, the doors were locked, but something happened in the institutionalization of children that interfered with their normal development.

I think one of the greatest challenges of long-term institutional living is that, for the most part, it's run by lay personnel, so the children remain in a constant state of uncertainty and anxiety because they are not parented. There's no guarantee that the primary caregiver who is an employee of the orphanage is not going to leave. These children, who are already vulnerable and often have symptoms of PTSD, have no certainty that the one person who is caring for them right now will remain. An orphanage that is losing employees and has large amounts of children to look after will choose the needs of the organization over the needs of the child. Lack of autonomy, lack of individuality, lack of connection, and lack of one-on-one care are often present. Subsequently, there are harmful effects on the children.

When we are dealing with young babies, infants, and neonates, obviously the formative years are incredibly important. They are the building blocks and the structures on which cognitive development will continue. Ideal best practice is for the child to remain with the parents or with a primary caregiver, a member of the extended family, or someone who will come when they cry, someone to meet their needs. What is needed is eye contact, touch, comfort, love, and an immediate response to hunger. We speak a lot about best-practice initiatives when child rearing and raising children, but ultimately children were designed to receive love. Sadly, in institutional settings, love from a committed parent is absent and we exchange love for management. These young infants, neonates, children under three, their building blocks and their foundational pathways are severely hindered in the absence of a primary caregiver and love.

I don't think there's a blanket response to how we can avoid the harmful consequences of institutionalized living. What I believe we can do is introduce a harm-reduction model that is evidence-based in its approach and is child-focused and trauma-informed. These harm-reduction framework models can be broken into three preventative subgroups. The first subgroup involves primary prevention measures. These may be provision and access to measures such as family planning and pre- and postnatal maternity health service. More examples include the elimination of poverty, the prevention of child exploitation and early marriages, the provision of and access to multidisciplinary support teams, and wraparound care for single parents. The prevention of trauma, abuse, and neglect within residential settings can be brought about through evidence-based, trauma-informed training for direct primary caregivers.

We have a model here in the UK that involves foster placements for both mother and baby. Let's say a young mom with three children is abandoned by her partner. He leaves and she's left home alone with three children. She does not have a career, and she does not have an education. How is she going to be self-sufficient and provide for her family? What we found in the UK is that the provision of foster homes for parent and child really helps. Usually within the first twelve months of provision of a safe place for mother and child, the mother can gain employment and find a secure home.

Secondary preventative measures are provision and access to professional-aid, community-based, family-care models. For example, reunification and deinstitutionalization when biological family options are feasible and safe and implementation of explicit measures to provide training for staff. We don't want to criticize the staffing institutions that are doing their best. I have found that most of them are sincerely there to help and to serve and they care deeply about children, but they lack professional evidence-based knowledge to best meet the holistic needs of the children in their care.

Knowledge is really a basis for helping build a stronger environment for these kids who have been placed there through adverse experiences in their lives. We want the best for them. We don't want them to grow up with weakened emotional development, psychosocial development, and even physical and cognitive development. Providing better training for the people who care for them is a key piece.

In addition, we are told in research that about 70 percent of all international residential facilities—orphanages—are actually funded partly or fully through the church. This is a great example of the magnitude of help churches provide, but it also raises the question as to why as the church we keep building orphanages when we have six decades of research to say that institutions are the least appropriate environment for child rearing.

This is a dial-up question I like to have with church leaders, with mission schools, or faith-based NGOs: can we, instead of raising funds for an orphanage, be strategic with our resources and instead support a child's family? For example, let's say there are one hundred children. Can we not break down what it would cost to house those hundred children and break that down into monthly payments for a longer time period? Say it costs twenty thousand dollars a year to run an orphanage. Can we provide two hundred dollars a month for a long-term investment in a child's family instead?

PARENTS AND YOUTH INTERNET SAFETY

More than ever, children, teens, and young adults are using the internet and social media as their primary tool for social interaction and schoolwork. We may think human trafficking is not happening in our own backyards; however, with the world on the internet, the world is our backyard. It is essential that church leaders, parents, and those who work with children be informed about the realities of youth and internet safety. We must educate our communities about the tactics of traffickers online, help prevent human trafficking, and be equipped to be part of the solution in ending it.

In 2019 and 2020 Thorn, a nonprofit organization that develops technology designed to protect children from sexual abuse, conducted some important studies revealing attitudes and threats kids in our society face that affect their vulnerability to trafficking and sexual exploitation. One of these threats is the proliferation of self-generated child sexual abuse material (SG-CSAM), sexual imagery of a child that appears to have been taken by the child in the image. This imagery can result from either a consensual or coercive experience. Consensual sharing of these images is often referred to by minors as "sexting" or "sharing nudes."[16] In coercive experiences, children are groomed or manipulated in some way to send nude images of themselves. Nonconsensual dissemination of intimate images (NCII) is the sharing of the SG-CSAM without the consent of the child who took the images.

One example is a thirteen-year-old boy who sends an intimate image to a girl he likes. Without asking him for permission, she shares it with friends. Another example is a ten-year-old girl who begins communicating with someone on social media, builds trust with that person, and shares a nude photo. Later the sex offender who was communicating with the girl shares the image on an online child pornography website.

In its research, Thorn learned that sharing intimate imagery with peers is common for kids in this digital age: "Sharing nudes and sexting is the new normal." The organization reports that in 2019, one in five girls aged thirteen to seventeen had shared nudes of themselves, and one in ten boys had as well. What's more, 40 percent of kids aged thirteen to seventeen agreed that "it's normal for people my age to share nudes with each other." Many kids said they had a positive experience when sharing nudes with peers, that doing this formed trust and helped them feel empowered.[17] For some kids sharing nudes is a form of sexual exploration and curiosity. As we might expect, other kids express shame and regret, while others share traumatic consequences. Regardless of its origins, once the material is shared with others, it is child sexual abuse.

This is important information for caring adults to be aware of and understand. Sexual exploration is considered developmentally normal for minors, and the online and physical worlds are connected for this generation. The problem is not their curiosity and experimentation; rather it is their vulnerability to the exploitation and harm that happens in the online world where there is little protection and predators are in abundance. Kids have grown up so connected to technology that it is woven into their daily communication. This close connection is not likely to change anytime soon. So rather than only being shocked and disgusted, we must also become informed and prepared to protect children in our society.

We know kids use many of the same social media platforms adults do, with new ones being created all the time. These include Instagram, Facebook, Snapchat, TikTok, and many others. Just like adults, kids use these platforms to connect to friends, meet new people, share information, and grow an online community. While there are plenty of positive interactions on these platforms, there are also plenty of negative ones. In Thorn's research, one of the most common negative incidents for kids "involves bullying or generally being made to feel uncomfortable," with 38 percent reporting this experience. Just behind this statistic is 33 percent of kids reporting "having had an online sexual interaction"—for example, sexting or being asked for or sent nude imagery.[18]

Girls ages thirteen to seventeen are three times more likely to be asked for a nude online than teen boys in the same age group. What is most concerning is that "minors are having online sexual interactions with individuals they believe to be adults and other minors at the same rate."[19] For minors who have had online sexual interaction, 26 percent didn't report it to anyone; either they thought it wasn't a big deal, they worried their report wouldn't remain anonymous, or they felt embarrassed. Of those who did report harmful online experiences, an overwhelming percentage reported to online safety organizations rather than to an individual offline.

Technology companies that build these social media platforms have an important role to play in protecting kids, but the reality is that they are either ignorant of the dangers or unwilling to create the changes necessary to protect our kids. There are organizations, such as Thorn and NCMEC, that are tackling these problems through research, advocacy, and legal channels.

What we know is that a strong network of community support is a major factor in teaching kids how to behave online. According to Thorn, seven in ten children between nine and seventeen have learned how to behave online from caregivers, and that number rises to eight in ten among younger children between ages nine to twelve.[20] It is important to start these conversations when children are young. By the time kids have reached high school, it is simply too late. If children are allowed to get online, watch videos on YouTube, or use any social media platform, they are old enough for this conversation.

How we communicate in these discussions is as important as the content of what we discuss. As we instruct, we also listen, suspending judgment or shame. We become the safe people our kids come to when they feel confused, threatened, or embarrassed about something, or when they are hurting. Our compassion and understanding could make all the difference to a child who simply feels embarrassed about something he or she saw or shared online instead of becoming a victim of trafficking. Thorn reports that concern about blame is the main reason children who have seen or sent SG-CSAM did not report the experience to an adult.[21] Even though kids say caregivers and other trusted adults teach them about online behavior, they don't say anything to them because they believe most people—including parents—will blame the person who took the image of him- or herself. It is crucial that adults build trust, and when kids do begin to share with them, they need to remain compassionate and resist blame and shame.

It is important for parents and caretakers to create rules for internet use with children and youth. The internet is ever-present, and while we know there are many positive benefits, we also know that dangers come along with it. We would not allow our children to play on the streets without teaching them basic road safety. The same principle needs to be true for the internet. We need to teach children basic safety when it comes to screen time. A good way to do that is by creating a set of rules for internet use. Consider the following questions and guidelines when composing internet use rules:

Who are children allowed to communicate with online? Parents and caretakers should know who their children are friends with on social media apps and who they are chatting with in chat groups. Anyone outside your child's social network who tries to contact or engage with your child online should be questioned immediately. We recommend parents and caretakers have access to all social media accounts and regularly monitor and discuss who is on there and what kinds of content are being posted and viewed. This might create pushback from teens, but the seriousness of this responsibility should outweigh any pushback.

When and for how long are children allowed to be on the internet? When are phones turned off at night and back on in the morning? How much time do children get on the computer each day and each week? They should never be getting up in the middle of the night to go online. Decide where they are allowed to use the internet—at a friend's house? At the public library? Only at home?

Under what circumstances are children allowed to be online? Discuss the reasons your child needs to be careful when online. Compare their need to be careful of strangers while playing outside to their need for caution while studying, gaming, or using the internet. Ensure that their time online is not a substitute for time together with you.

Where is screen time allowed to take place? All computers and electronic devices (including smartphones) with internet access should be located in the home where parents and guardians can supervise. Computers and electronic devices with internet access should not be located in bedrooms or other places where adults cannot supervise. Locating electronic devices in bedrooms and other low-traffic areas of the house creates risk. As a parent, you would never leave your child unsupervised with a stranger. They could get hurt. The same mentality applies for supervising children during internet use.

What sites are your children visiting? Children are not completely safe even if they only visit child-friendly chat rooms. Nothing is completely childproof on the web. People wanting to entice children usually frequent child-friendly chat rooms looking for victims. They also use false profiles to engage and create an online relationship with children.

Check your children's browser history and phone texts. Part of protecting your children is knowing where and what sites they have accessed online—this includes computers, smartphones, gaming systems, and any other electronic devices with internet access. This simple step can prevent real harm from happening to children in the long term. You do not need to do this covertly; instead, sit down with your children and have them show you the sites they are accessing. It will help you know where children are going on the web and help you identify if your child has stumbled onto a porn site while doing homework or accessing a children's website. Also, read through the texts being sent between your children and their friends. This will help ensure that they are only texting with people they know and are not being asked to do something inappropriate. The more regularly you do this with your child or teenager, the more it becomes a regular part of the responsibility that comes with having technology.

What will you do in a potentially dangerous situation? Make a plan with your children should someone request their phone number or ask to meet in person. We already tell our children and youth not to talk to, share personal information with, or go anywhere with strangers without telling us. This principle should be applied online. Children and youth should never talk to someone they don't already know from their social network. All new online acquaintances and friends should be shared with and approved by parents. It is important for parents to monitor this closely, as predators often pretend to be a child or youth online to lure them into conversation and a relationship. It should be stressed with children and youth that they should never share their phone numbers, addresses, or any personal information online.

What are your children's screen usernames and email addresses? Most children want to create usernames and email addresses they consider to be cool and reflective of them. But sometimes these types of usernames and email addresses can tell online predators personal details about a child or youth. Refrain from using actual names, year of birth, age, or any phrases that would hint at their being a child.

How will you address sexual interactions or exchanges involving nudity? "Sextortion" takes many different forms, but basically it is a threat to expose sexual images in order to make a person do something. These threats can come from strangers online or from former romantic partners who attempt to harass, embarrass, or control victims.[22] Talk with your child or youth about the consequences of sexting—that this act could lead to sextortion. Children's and youths' brains are still developing, so they may not be able to understand the risks or long-term repercussions of this choice. Checking a young person's text messages regularly and supervising the use of the internet and electronics helps decrease these risks.

Once an image is sent, those looking to exploit children will threaten to expose them, often demanding more images in the process. This kind of exploitation is a powerful trap and unlikely to stop without intervention from law enforcement. Have a discussion with your child or youth about sextortion in advance to protect them and help them feel comfortable telling you if this happens to them. They need to know they can come to you (or a trusted adult) right away if they have been asked to sext, without fear of consequences. Save all information and content and make sure to report the incident immediately to law enforcement. Suspend shock, disappointment, or shame if you find that a child has shared a nude willingly. Building trust and being a safe adult to turn to is the goal, and children of all ages are very aware of when they are being shamed.

What role does the internet play in your life with children? Spend time with your children and teens doing activities that build trust. Create and prioritize activities that affirm and communicate a sincere interest in who they are. Ensure that your family entertainment is not restricted to the virtual world and that it includes creative bonding, joy, and support for one another.

The church can be a strong advocate in protecting minors of all ages. Anyone working with children or youth in a church can be trained to understand how minors are vulnerable to exploitation online. By training employees and volunteers, we reinforce the work parents might be doing at home in protecting their kids. For those kids who don't have parents paying attention to online risk, a church volunteer might notice something a child shares that is concerning and that needs to be addressed. Church employees or volunteers are in a position to educate a minor in cyber exploitation.

In the United States, the National Center for Missing and Exploited Children (NCMEC) is one of the most important resources to be aware of (see missingkids.org). NCMEC is the national learning house and comprehensive reporting center for all issues related to the prevention of and recovery from child victimization. NCMEC works with families, victims, private industry, law enforcement, and the public to assist with preventing child abductions, recovering missing children, and providing services to deter and combat child sexual exploitation. Internationally, refer to the International Center for Missing and Exploited Children.

Since 1998, NCMEC also has operated the CyberTipline, a tool for the public and electronic service providers to report suspected online child sexual exploitation and child sexual image materials. Additionally, resources for parents, educators, and the community are free in the NetSmartz section of their website (missingkids.org/netsmartz/resources).

Remember the public health model—predict, protect, practice? When you teach your child to brush their teeth, they do it every day. NetSmartz materials are age-appropriate prevention training tools that are available for regular use in your home, your classroom, and even your children's ministry. They are developed through a public-private partnership with the FBI, so the latest technology studies are regularly updated.

SEXTORTION RED FLAGS

People involved in "sextortion" of children often

1. Approach a child on social media after using it to learn about the child's interests, friends, school, family, and so on
2. Intentionally move their communications with the child from one online platform to another (e.g., moving from social media to private video chat or messaging apps)
3. Use tactics to coerce a child, including
   - Reciprocation ("I'll show you if you show me")
   - Initially offering something to the child, such as money or drugs, in exchange for sexually explicit photos or videos
   - Pretending to work for a modeling agency to obtain sexual images of the child
   - Developing a bond with the child by establishing a friendship or romantic relationship
   - Secretly recording sexually explicit videos of the child during video chats
   - Physically threatening to hurt or sexually assault the child or the child's family members
   - Using multiple online identities to contact a child
   - Pretending to be younger or a member of the opposite sex
   - Accessing the child's online account without authorization and stealing sexual images or videos of the child
   - Threatening to create sexual images or videos of the child using digital-editing tools
   - Threatening to commit suicide if the child does not provide sexual images or videos
   - Saving sexually explicit conversations with the child and threatening to post them online[23]

COVID-19 AND YOUTH

As with other natural disasters and national or global crises, Covid-19 increased vulnerability to trafficking, particularly for children. Traffickers are entrepreneurial, always adjusting their techniques to fit the circumstances and the demand. Covid-19 created an environment where people were locked down and spending more time at home and in their room and on screens. As a result, traffickers adjusted their methods of getting their product to consumers.

NCMEC is aware that child predators and traffickers are holding discussions on the dark web about the opportunity Covid-19 presents to entice more children to produce sexually explicit material. "COVID-19 has presented challenges and opportunities in the fight against child sexual exploitation. In the first quarter of 2020, we experienced an explosion in reporting to our CyberTipline from both the public and electronic service providers," says John Shehan, vice president of NCMEC's Exploited Children Division.[24] In addition, some traffickers are "now offering options for subscription-based services in which buyers pay to access online images and videos of the child."[25] NCMEC experienced a 98.66 percent increase in online enticement reports between January and September 2020 versus the same time period in 2019.[26]

Today more than ever, parents—and all individuals who work with children—need to be diligent, openly and age-appropriately discussing the reality of what is happening online with exploitation and trafficking. They need to regularly monitor the technology of minors of any age. Pay attention if a minor is spending more time on their phone, online, or on their computer, especially at night. We recommend that no technological devices be used in isolation, including bedrooms or home offices where there is no accountability.

BUILD A SAFETY FENCE: FENCEPOSTS

- Identify where the model of predict, protect, practice is being used in your anti-human-trafficking efforts and, if it is not, work to incorporate this model into any programs that involve children.
- Support foster youth. This may look like partnering with a foster care program in your area or connecting congregants who are considering being foster parents. Support families who are already foster parents.
- Partner with programs that mentor and support youth in the greater community who might not attend your particular youth group. These might include a local Boys and Girls Club, YMCA, or the Big Brother/Big Sister program.

- Utilize internet safety resources from websites such as Common Sense Media (commonsensemedia.org). Use NCMEC/NetSmartz materials. These materials are constantly upgraded and a good use of your taxpayer money.
- Create a program or host events for parents, families, and those who work with children to provide youth internet safety tools and training.
- If you're concerned about abuse or neglect of a child in your community, contact the National Child Abuse Hotline number, 1-800-422-4453, or visit the Child Help Hotline online (childhlephotline.org).
- If you're concerned a child may be a victim of online exploitation, report it immediately to the CyberTipline (missingkids.org/gethelpnow/cybertipline) or call 1-800-THE-LOST.

THE REFUGEE AND IMMIGRANT

> For I was hungry and you gave me something to eat, I was thirsty and you gave me something to drink, I was a stranger and you invited me in. (Matthew 25:35)

Told they will have well-paying jobs when they arrive in the United States, thousands of immigrants and refugees are tricked into forced labor annually. Traffickers often deceive these people by offering half-truths, promising the individual will work at a restaurant or in a hotel. Once these people begin working, they are held captive either through never-ending debt or simple physical immobility. Without knowing the language or having someone to trust and under constant threat of physical violence, these people work in the background of our public businesses every day.

Regardless of where we stand politically as individuals regarding how our nation or community should care for immigrants and refugees, as Christians we know we must. The "how" may look different in our varying perspectives, but there should be no question that God calls us to care for the foreigner. It is good to reflect on the fact that we are also foreigners. We may have citizenship in a nation on earth, but our ultimate citizenship is in heaven.

As Christians we are not of this world. Our biblical ancestry is rooted in the fact that we are aliens, immigrants fleeing from Egypt and trying to reach the Promised Land. Millions of people today are also fleeing their current land to find not a Promised Land but a land where they are safe, a land where there is food, a land where there is no war, a land where they might find a job to provide for their families. We are all made in the image of God, and what we do—or do not do—to the least among us we do to God: "Truly I tell you, whatever you did for one of the least of these brothers and sisters of mine, you did for me" (Matthew 25:40).

As followers of Jesus Christ, we set aside political agendas, the need to have a perfect response, and the desire to solve all the immigration and refugee struggles in our country, and we acknowledge that all people are made in the image of God and worthy of our love and care. We may flush out our understanding in different ways, but let us be clear in acknowledging that our Lord God commands us to love and care for others. This has been written in Scripture from the creation of humankind, the identity of the people of Israel, and the call to community of the early church.

> I am a foreigner and stranger among you. Sell me some property for a burial site here so I can bury my dead. (Genesis 23:4)

> You are to love those who are foreigners, for you yourselves were foreigners in Egypt. (Deuteronomy 10:19)

> The foreigner residing among you must be treated as your native-born. Love them as yourself, for you were foreigners in Egypt. I am the LORD your God. (Leviticus 19:34)

> "Cursed is anyone who withholds justice from the foreigner, the fatherless or the widow."
> Then all the people shall say, "Amen!" (Deuteronomy 27:19)

We acknowledge that we are called by God to care for the foreigner, the immigrant, and the refugee, but understanding the problem and the best course of action for care is difficult and complicated. Human conflict and violence are the main reasons for mass migration. By the end of 2014, war, violence, and persecution had led to one in every 122 people in the world becoming a refugee, becoming displaced, or seeking asylum.[27] The United Nations Refugee Agency (UNHCR) reports that the level of worldwide displacement has never been higher, with one percent of the world's population now displaced from their homes. That is one in over ninety-seven people without a land to call home. A UNHCR Global Trends report shows that of the 79.5 million people who were displaced at the end of 2018, 45.7 million had fled to different regions of their own countries. The rest had been displaced in other countries: 4.2 million were awaiting the results of asylum requests, 29.6 million were refugees, and others had been forcibly driven out of their country.[28]

For purposes of clarity, let's look at the difference between an immigrant and a refugee. An immigrant is someone who chooses to resettle to another country. Each country has different laws, or lack thereof, for people who choose to enter that country. In the United States there is a legal process for immigrants to seek legal residency and eventual citizenship. Due to a variety of reasons, however, many immigrants don't have such legal status and are subsequently undocumented. Undocumented immigrants are subject to deportation from the United States. There are approximately 11 million undocumented immigrants in the United States, a problem this nation has struggled to reform for decades.[29] Complicated and broken visa systems, along with strong economic profitability from the use of undocumented immigrant workers, add to the broken system, making caring for people and preventing exploitation and trafficking difficult.

An immigrant is different from a refugee. According to the United Nations Refugee Agency, a refugee is "someone who has been forced to flee his or her home country due to war, persecution, or violence. A refugee has a valid fear of persecution for reasons of race, religion, nationality, political opinion, or membership of a particular social group. A refugee most likely cannot return home or is afraid to do so due to violence. War and ethnic, tribal, and religious violence are leading causes of refugees fleeing their countries."[30]

In the United States refugees can apply for asylum, a process that can take many years. Applicants have to prove that if they return to their home country, they will be harmed due to their race, religion, nationality, political opinion, or membership of a particular social group. This can get complicated when there is an outburst of violence like we have seen lately in Central America. The recent overwhelming number of immigrants from

Central America—particularly Honduras, Guatemala, and El Salvador—have come to the United States–Mexico border fleeing drug- and gang-related violence in their home countries.

To receive refugee status, a person must be specifically targeted because of one of the required attributes of race, religion, and so on. This is where the problem gets very complicated. Every case is different, and in 2008 President George W. Bush signed a law that put children into a special class. The Trafficking Victims Protection Reauthorization Act (TVPRA) of 2008 included provisions for unaccompanied migrant children who are vulnerable to trafficking en route or while in the United States. This law ensured that children who came to the United States would get a full immigration hearing instead of being turned away or sent back. This hearing determines whether the children have a valid claim for asylum.

Another note of distinction is the difference between refugee and asylum seeker. According to the National Association of Social Workers, an asylum seeker is "an individual who has left her or his country because of a well-founded fear of persecution due to race, religion, nationality, political opinion, or membership of a particular social group but has not been granted asylum status in the United States. People seeking asylum must go through the immigration court system before they can be considered for asylum, whereas refugees already have legal status when they arrive in the United States."[31] There are also special cases where Iraqi and Afghan translators and interpreters working for the United States military who meet certain requirements can qualify for the special immigrant visa and receive refugee benefits as well.

Each refugee must undergo a rigorous interviewing process to ensure they meet the required definition of refugee. In the United States this means they must prove their case of "well-founded fear" of going back to their home country. They must also not have settled in any other country. Then there is an extensive screening and security clearance process conducted by regional refugee coordinators who oversee resettlement support centers (RSCs). They can deny an application for refugee resettlement status on "health-related grounds, criminal grounds, and security grounds. They may also be denied for polygamy, misrepresentation of facts on visa applications, smuggling, and previous deportations."[32]

Once a refugee has been conditionally accepted for resettlement, the RSC sends a request for placement to the United States, and the refugee processing center works with private voluntary refugee resettlement agencies to determine where the refugee will live. Before arriving in the United States, all approved refugees undergo health screenings to prevent those with contagious diseases from entering. Most also undergo a cultural orientation before their arrival as well.

Each country that accepts refugees has a different resettlement process. In the United States refugees are resettled through national resettlement agencies. There are nine refugee resettlement agencies in the United States that are contracted by the federal government to assist refugees. Case managers assist the newly arrived refugees with a variety of services to help them adjust to their new communities and facilitate their transitions to become productive future citizens of the United States. Currently the nine refugee resettlement agencies in the United States are

- Church World Service
- Ethiopian Community Development Council
- Episcopal Migration Ministries
- Hebrew Immigrant Aid Society
- International Rescue Committee
- US Committee for Refugees and Immigrants
- Lutheran Immigration and Refugee Services
- United States Conference of Catholic Bishops
- World Relief Corporation

As you can see, there are many Christian-based refugee resettlement agencies. If you and your church are interested in or open to learning more or getting involved with immigrants and refugees, choose a refugee resettlement agency to support. Many have worked with these agencies in some capacity and have seen their work firsthand. Find out which agencies work in your area so your church can get informed and connected to assisting refugees in your community. Also, a church can begin to build friendships among diverse cultures and faiths. This can help elevate our understanding of the "other" and strengthen our listening and learning skills.

BUILDING TRUST WITH IMMIGRANTS AND REFUGEES

Rachel Parker, Anti-Human-Trafficking Program Manager, World Relief

Building trusting relationships with refugees and immigrants in our communities is important to serving them well. Individuals coming from other countries may not have any experience with a service infrastructure in their home nations, and when as organizations or churches we offer resources, we sometimes feel like we are hitting a wall, and we don't understand why.

It is helpful to ask what a give-and-take relationship looks like for someone in that situation. In some cultures, if you provide a person with something of value, they owe you something back. Maybe they have been in an exploitive relationship involving either labor or sex trafficking. Being offered services can be a very scary situation for them.

I worked with someone from China who wanted to know what my stake was in helping her. How was I going to profit? I had to explain, "I get paid to help you, and this is how I think I can help from what you're telling me. Let me explain what I'm going to do. We'll go to a coffee shop and talk about your goals."

Something else we have encountered at World Relief is that receiving help can make men feel emasculated and even more victimized. We often see people at the lowest point in their life, and it is tempting to swoop in and help them. Some immigrants and refugees may stand back and let us do the work we've identified, but they may not actually want us to. And it may not ultimately be what they see as their priority. It is important to help them take ownership of their plan and get buy-in from the refugees we are serving.

Vulnerabilities in refugee and immigrant communities are varied, so we focus on primary-level prevention. We worked with a couple of gentlemen who had come into the country under work visas. When they got to their workplace, they discovered that what they'd been told they would be doing was not true—it was a situation of fraud. The fake employers attempted to coerce them into cooperation, saying, "I know where your family is." Fortunately, they had received information about human trafficking and labor trafficking. One of the gentlemen knew of the national hotline number, and he called and got himself out of that situation.

Another thing to consider is who offers pro bono or affordable legal assistance for immigrants and refugees in your area. A woman from North Carolina wrote a book on how to build your practice by granting T visas (a special humanitarian visa) to refugees, and we have seen T visa application fees ranging from $9,000 to $19,000. That's victimizing the victims. If you have an outreach to ethnic groups and refugees in your area, make sure you're collaborating with other networks in your community so if you see something suspicious, you know who to connect with and provide support.

Local churches that want to work with immigrant populations need to have ties to those immigrant populations. We need to get out and connect with the diverse communities present in our midst. The people we seek to help should be represented in our leadership as well, because we won't understand the culture and all of the influences on it. English as a second language (ESL) classes are a great place for churches to start, and so is childcare. Currently, we are struggling to help two clients who are single parents. They have found jobs, but they do not have anyone to watch their children.

BUILD A SAFETY FENCE: FENCEPOSTS

- Educate yourself and your church about the immigrant and refugee populations in your area.
- Build real and authentic relationships based on listening and trust in order to serve them well.
- Collaborate with others in your area who are serving refugees and immigrants and join in the work they are already doing.
- Begin ESL classes or offer childcare to these populations in your church building.

5

PROSECUTION

PEOPLE IN PLACES OF POWER

All that is required for evil to triumph is for good men to do nothing.

EDMUND BURKE

Truth compels people of goodwill to act; and because all that is necessary for the triumph of evil is for good people to do nothing, the end is near for the perpetrators of injustice when the truth compels good people to do something, especially good people in places of power.

GARY HAUGEN

POVERTY, IMMIGRATION STATUS, lack of education, lack of stable family life, natural disasters, and lack of job opportunities all play a part in how vulnerable a person is to being trafficked. But while these push-pull factors may contribute to vulnerability, they are not the root cause. According to John Cotton Richmond, cofounder of the Human Trafficking Institute and ambassador-at-large with the US State Department's Office to Monitor and Combat Trafficking in Persons, "The root cause of human trafficking is the trafficker."[1]

The trafficker—the person choosing to exploit, coerce, or force another person into work or sex—is ultimately the reason the crime of trafficking exists. Stop the trafficker; stop human trafficking. People's circumstances contribute to their accessibility and the ease with which traffickers lure, manipulate, or force them into work, but "towering about all these significant challenges in human trafficking is the traffickers' willful decision to profit by compelling people to work or prostitute," Richmond says.[2] Traffickers are the perpetrators who actively plan and scheme to break the law because it is profitable for them to do so.

For traffickers, financial profitability outweighs risk. As with most business models, money is the motive. We know from Scripture that "the love of money is a root of all kinds of evil" (1 Timothy 6:10). Unlike other problems that negatively overwhelm vulnerable populations, such as natural disasters or viruses, human trafficking is one that can be prevented. Human trafficking is the direct result of a choice another human being makes. Traffickers deliberately choose to exploit another human being for money. This is an important piece of the puzzle when we are studying the local and global problem of human trafficking and how best to put an end to it.

This fact informs our understanding of the significance of prosecution and allows us to experience real hope for the end of human trafficking. We must not only understand survivor needs and care for victims; our efforts must include stopping the people who instigate and benefit from the crime.

In the last twenty years we have gained greater understanding of the profile of traffickers and what motivates them to exploit others. Traffickers come in all shapes and sizes, meaning they do not fit into any specific category of gender, race, or economic status. But the one unifying characteristic they all have in common is their primary motivation: to make money. Some traffickers may make money through commercial sex trafficking in a brothel or massage business; others make money through labor trafficking in a restaurant, hotel, or agriculture business. Why do these people exploit others? The answer is painfully simple: because they can. Why pay someone for their services when you can force them and make more money?

Historically, traffickers have faced little risk in exploiting others in this way. When profit is the bottom line, when more is better, when the risk of getting caught is slim, and when the consequences for getting caught are negligible, then there is very little to lose for the trafficker. Low risk, high profits. The perfect business model.

If we look at traffickers the way we would any other businessperson, we can see their motivation more clearly. For instance, labor traffickers could hire people to work for them by paying a competitive wage, economically incentivizing them to keep them from going somewhere else, or they could use force, threats, violence, coercion, or some combination of those things to compel them to work and prevent them from leaving. "If there is no practical consequence for engaging in coercive schemes, then traffickers realize they are just going to make more money," says Victor Boutros, CEO of the Human Trafficking Institute.[3]

The business of human trafficking grows exponentially where enforcement of laws is low. Where there is little to no meaningful risk that a person will be caught, traffickers operate freely. Where laws are enforced and where this crime is punished severely, human trafficking is reduced significantly. "Traffickers may have varying levels of risk tolerance, but if enforcement risk is effectively zero, then they're all engaging in the crime because it is worth it, even if their risk tolerance is low," Boutros says. "If we can increase law enforcement risk even modestly, we can thin out a significant group of risk-sensitive traffickers who are only willing to engage in the crime if they know there's a zero chance they will get in trouble for it."[4]

In 2005, the International Justice Mission launched an anti-sex-trafficking project in Cebu, Philippines, focused on increased training for law enforcement. This program, given the name Project Lantern, has been incredibly successful, resulting in a 70 percent decrease in trafficking after a five-year investment in the region. This outcome provides clear evidence that training for officers can significantly decrease trafficking in a community.[5]

This is why it is so important not only to understand the problem of human trafficking and how to adequately care and support survivors, but also to know how crucial law enforcement and prosecution of human traffickers are to the eliminating this crime altogether. Stopping the trafficker from making a decision to force, coerce, threaten, or manipulate people could prevent a future vulnerable population from being exploited in the first place. But to do this is not simple. Human traffickers adapt and adjust to the risks, culture, and demand in a community.

One of the things we can do as pastors, church leaders, and community leaders is to understand what lane we are in. Unless we have a law degree or are in law enforcement, those sectors of anti-trafficking work are not our lane. Staying in our lane and understanding how to support others in their lanes is one of the most important things we as the church can do. By understanding our lane, we honor the people who have authority and who are investigating crimes and building legal cases.

Years ago, when Sandie went to Wisconsin to do a training for a large church, she asked that they invite representatives of their local law enforcement agencies to speak during the event. According to Joelene Taylor at Journey Church, building communication and trust with law enforcement made a huge difference in this church's ability to equip themselves and those in their community, strengthen their anti-trafficking work, and, ultimately, build their community relationships and capacity for justice work upstream in prevention.

We all have different roles, and none of us has everything needed to fight trafficking in our toolbox. By understanding our roles and engaging the broader community, we can be more effective in preventing trafficking from occurring and better meet the needs of survivors. For example, if law enforcement agents are working on an investigation and attorneys are building a case but the victims in the case do not feel safe and supported, the case won't be successful because the victims won't testify. The church can play an important role here. It can support law enforcement in making sure they have everything they need for that case, respect them, and remain supportive in love and care for the victim.

People in our churches—even those with law enforcement backgrounds—should not conduct trainings on finding trafficking victims in our communities independent of law enforcement officials. We have many stories we could share, but we will highlight a specific one to create better understanding of this issue. When Sandie was administrator for the Orange County Human Trafficking Task Force, the FBI called and asked her to speak to a community group that, after being "trained," had started investigating a brothel close to where some of the people lived. The FBI was already investigating this location and had identified college students from this community group that they had observed in their stakeout the weekend before. The FBI had been doing surveillance for weeks following particular protocols and the laws required for such an investigation. When Sandie went to speak to this group, one of the girls had on an outfit as if she were going out to a club or, in this case, someone who might be seen in the brothel the FBI was investigating. Sandie had to tell these well-intentioned college students that if they were attempting their own undercover investigation and in the brothel, they would be arrested by the FBI and could not be bailed out for at least twenty-four hours.

This is just one of many stories where laypeople with good intentions could have botched an active human trafficking investigation because they acted on their own without cooperation from government agencies and law enforcement. This kind of well-meaning but ill-informed action not only costs communities thousands of dollars of wasted resources and time, but it costs potential victims lasting justice, and it costs the church its witness and reputation.

As church leaders we might not totally understand all the details of a situation, but we need to respect those in authority in our community and find ways to support them. If our local law enforcement agencies are not already trained or connected to a human trafficking task force, we can advocate for local leaders to strengthen their response. Many law enforcement agencies are stretched to capacity, but they will often be willing to engage with your community, especially to partner in community awareness activities. Many crimes involved with human trafficking are activities they are already policing. Education and training take time, so being supportive of our law enforcement agencies is always best practice for long-term community solutions.

When we first learn about the realities of human trafficking, we might be deeply moved, experiencing significant anger or grief. The evil of this crime can feel overwhelming. We might feel compelled to do something—to rescue, to act—and this feeling may actually be prompted by the Holy Spirit. Yet wisdom reminds us that an effective and even transformational response requires not emotion but rather thoughtfulness and a strategic approach. Understanding the problem, assessing community and individual resources, building relationships with community and government agencies, investigating and building cases, and undertaking the restorative work of healing for survivors take time. They take longer than emotions last, as important as those are in getting us started and reminding us why we do this. Justice takes time. And this is justice work.

We do not always get to see the fullness of justice at work in individual cases, just as we do not always see the fullness of justice in other areas, although we recognize God is still at work here on earth. We will not always see the problem being remedied when law enforcement is behind the scenes building a case. We have to trust that the authority given to them is being carried out. We have to trust they are doing their jobs just as we are.

The church can specifically support law enforcement through prayer and relationship building. Sometimes cases will not look like justice. Maybe a child was moved back home to her parents who were complicit in the trafficking. Times like this will be tough on us, no doubt, because we know there should be a more just outcome. But this might be the right conclusion within the laws that are in place at the time and considering the evidence available.

PROSECUTION CASE STUDY

***Juliet Oliver, Deputy District Attorney, Human Exploitation and Trafficking Unit, Orange County District Attorney's Office*[6]**

In June of 2016, Jane Doe, who was thirteen years old, was walking "the track," a street known for prostitution, in a city in Orange County, California, when she was contacted by law enforcement. She was contacted because of her clothing, the time of night, and, most importantly, because she looked very young. She was asked if she was engaging in prostitution. She initially lied and said no, she wasn't, but later admitted to engaging in the activity. She told law enforcement she was engaging in this activity on her own initiative but identified a "friend" who had brought her to that particular location. Credit to some very good investigative work, law enforcement continued to talk to her about this particular "friend." This young girl eventually led them to this individual, who was parked in a car.[7]

This individual, just less than a mile away, had been engaging in text messages with Jane Doe while she was walking the track.[8] This was an important link because traffickers utilize text messaging fairly routinely to communicate with those working for them. Officers could see on Jane Doe's phone that someone by the name of John kept calling her. They suspected that this might be a trafficker attempting to contact her, potentially knowing she was being contacted by law enforcement. With her consent, they ultimately seized the phone that Jane Doe was using.

Despite the fact that she called "John" simply a friend, it was immediately obvious in those text messages that he was trafficking her. She was talking about specific "dates" she was going on, "dates" being a word used in the pimping pattern context to refer to the exchange of a sexual act for money. He was encouraging her to do all sorts of things sexually, and it was clear that he knew she was underage.

Based on those messages, he was arrested that night. Jane Doe was actually arrested that night as well. Not for prostitution activities, because in California we cannot arrest a minor for prostitution due to the decriminalization statutes, but for lying to a police officer, having ultimately not given her correct age and date of birth, which is also very common for minors who are being trafficked. It was learned that she was on the run and was a missing juvenile. She was placed into juvenile hall. Of course, it was horribly unfortunate that she had to be in juvenile hall, but there was no other secure facility to place her in.

When she talked to police officers, even after "John" was identified and arrested, becoming a defendant in a criminal case, she was unwilling to talk about him as a pimp or a trafficker. Based on text messages, it was clear they had engaged in sexual activity. Yet she denied any of that and completely shut down to law enforcement, refusing to give any additional information. Along with members of the Orange County Human Trafficking Task Force, I went the following morning to juvenile hall to talk to her and discovered she had a black eye that had been undetected in the middle of the night due to lighting conditions. It was only later that these injuries were observed and photographed. She did not want to discuss who was responsible for that injury, and she lied about it in general.

Approximately two weeks later, after continued meetings with her and the building of some rapport, she did admit the defendant was trafficking her and that they had engaged in multiple different sex acts together. He had been trafficking her for about a month in various counties throughout California, and he had physically assaulted her countless times over the course of that month.

Human trafficking of a minor is penal code section 236.1 B1, and it carries a maximum exposure and state prison time of twelve years. However, we have what we refer to, at least in our county, as the "force enhancement," which is penal code section 236.1 B2. This is when we see elements of force, fear, duress, coercion, menace, and the threat of unlawful injury. Then we can file force enhancement, which elevates the defendant's prison exposure, causing them to face a minimum of fifteen years to life in state prison.

Someone can be guilty of trafficking by merely attempting to cause a child to engage in prostitution activity with an intent to pander them. It's a low standard as far as the type of conduct that falls into trafficking of a minor. Of course, it's very important for us to have an effect on the human trafficking epidemic in our county and across the country. But the law recognizes that if the activity includes force, fear, duress, and the like, then an enhancement is called for. The unfortunate reality is that the force enhancement typically requires a cooperative victim. And that is very unusual in our world.

Unfortunately, the victims of trafficking typically have tragic and trauma-ridden histories that have led them to distrust police. Unless we have extrinsic evidence, we usually will not be able to file the force enhancement. For example, if Jane Doe had not had that black eye the day law enforcement pulled her over, we wouldn't have known to ask those questions. She probably would have been asked, "Is he physical with you?" and she would have said no. And that would have been the end of it.

This trafficker was successfully prosecuted, but only because of many different agencies and partners that came together to ensure the victim's safety and ensure that he would never victimize her again. This case was successful because of two things: collaborative efforts outside the county and, of course, within the county. Jane Doe had previously been contacted by law enforcement and social services outside of Orange County. Because she was a minor, she of course had a social worker, and that social worker was aware of her contact in a different county. When we received our case the very morning the defendant was in custody and Jane Doe was in juvenile hall, I received a call from a social worker who already knew Jane Doe had been contacted by law enforcement here at Orange County.

She proceeded to tell me about Jane Doe's history and being contacted by law enforcement there. I immediately contacted the district attorney and the investigator involved in that law enforcement contact in that county. They told me how Jane Doe had spoken with them and talked about a trafficker named John who was physically abusive with her. And she had talked about different facts that made us know it was specifically John Calhoun, my defendant. Based on the statements and information I received from the other county, I was immediately able to file the force enhancement, even though Jane Doe, sitting in juvenile hall, was denying that he was responsible for her physical abuse. That is an example of the outside collaboration.

Jane Doe was seen by Grace Court, the court here in Orange County. She was first seen by a judge and was appointed a public defender. I was there. The investigating officer was there, and we began to meet and learn about Jane Doe. We all worked together to try to encourage her, when she left juvenile hall, to stay in a placement setting where she would be assigned. Unfortunately—again, this is very common in our field—she was not interested in staying put in a particular location. She already had a history of being a habitual runaway. She continued to do this through the course of our investigation and prosecution. She admitted to telling people what they wanted to hear to get where she needed to go, because she didn't expect to see any of these people again, whether it was a social worker, a law enforcement officer, or a probation officer coming to visit her in the hall. This was her survival mechanism.

One of the things I wanted to show her was that we were not typical adults. We were the ones who were going to continue to be there and meet her wherever she was every single time. That if she ran, we would be there when she was ready to come back. If she ran, we were the ones she could call and say, "I want to come back" or "I'm out on the track and I need help." And we would continue to show up.

That is truly what happened over the course of her experience with the justice system while the case was being prosecuted. And law enforcement did continue to pursue her every single time she ran. If a warrant was put out for her, the Orange County Human Trafficking Task Force specifically went out and looked for her. And every time she was picked up, she was so pleasantly surprised.

Of course, as a thirteen-year-old minor on the run she was frustrated, but she ultimately was always happy these people had come and found her. She was amazed that law enforcement had committed to finding her and caring for her. And because of her experience in Grace Court, every time law enforcement contacted her, we brought her back to Grace Court, which allowed her to sit with the same prosecutor, myself, the same local social worker, the same victim advocate, and the same judge who was already familiar with her history.

We then could move forward together with her, as opposed to being a new set of faces to whom she would say whatever she needed to say to get by. It was that collaborative effort with social services, the Orange County Human Trafficking Task Force, the court system, the public defender's office, and our wonderful victim advocacy partners, Waymakers. All of us together continuing to wrap around her ultimately led to the successful prosecution of the trafficker and ultimately to Jane Doe's success as well. Now she is doing very, very well.

ROLE OF THE CHURCH IN PROSECUTION

This case demonstrates a variety of agencies working together, which makes this a good place to pause and ask where the church could support and provide transformative aid in situations like this. Could it engage in its community to help prevent something like this from even happening? Could it create a loving community to support the child and her case worker? Could it provide education on what fuels the demand for thirteen-year-olds in the first place? Every state has certification programs for those who work with victims of domestic violence and sexual abuse. The church should be flocking to these trainings, getting the proper education to be on the frontlines alongside these agencies. Many states have victim advocate roles available, where volunteers are on call to go emergency rooms and court cases when a victim is discovered.

One of the things about prosecution that's important to understand is the victim-offender cycle. Similar to other forms of trauma-bonding behavior, victims will often go back to their offender. Part of the reason is that they feel isolated; they may be in a strange place with no faces they recognize. And as beautiful as the place may look with new curtains and bedspreads, it is unfamiliar and possibly disorienting. It is not permanent. It is not a home. As distorted as it might seem, there is much evidence that victims of trafficking often go back to the people who sold them, whether that is a biological family or the family they just left. It might be a broken home, but to them it is the only home or the last home they knew. Perhaps the church could work to create safe spaces for victims and safe relationships for these individuals.

As we learned in chapter four in our discussion of trauma, victims of human trafficking, just as with victims of any extreme violence or sexual violence, often suffer injuries that are not visible. The trauma victims suffer goes beyond the initial assault and may linger through long-lasting psychological wounds. There is a general acknowledgment that people who suffer trauma in war or other situations of extreme violence such as shootings or stabbings experience lingering psychological distress.[9]

Sexual assault committed by strangers also may trigger long-lasting symptoms of trauma. When victims of trafficking are not adequately cared for, they often shut down and can be discouraged from seeking help. When they do come forward, victims can become retraumatized if the people they interact with—even those who are trying to help—minimize, criticize, blame, or are simply inadequately trained to respond with sensitivity to the psychological nature of their injuries. Christians who acquire state certification would have the opportunity to speak helpfully and love these survivors.

Supporting victims does not need to be a job just for law enforcement or government agencies. The church is the hope of the world and, if educated on trauma and victimization, it is the ideal place and group of people to provide loving support for survivors—it is a place where survivors can begin to make new friendships and build community.

MOVE UPSTREAM

John Cotton Richmond, Ambassador-at-Large,
Office to Monitor and Combat Trafficking in Persons, and
Founder of the Human Trafficking Institute[10]

The Human Trafficking Institute exists to decimate modern slavery at its source by empowering police and prosecutors to stop traffickers. Working inside criminal justice systems, the institute provides the embedded experts, world-class training, investigative resources, and evidence-based research necessary to free victims.[11]

One of the things we began to notice at the Human Trafficking Institute is that most of our anti-human-trafficking activities fall into one of three categories. The first category is making people less vulnerable to traffickers. We do things like awareness campaigns to let people know their rights and try to do poverty alleviation to help people have fewer felt needs so traffickers have fewer things to exploit. But we have noticed that this has had little impact on the trafficker's business model. Even if our efforts at vulnerability reduction are wildly successful, there are still two billion people living on less than two dollars a day, and here at home we have people aging out of a fractured foster care system for traffickers to exploit.

Another category is caring for survivors. Many of our activities go toward survivor care, which is essential and needs to be increased. We have been looking at trauma-informed counseling for victims, building job skills, providing medical care, removing tattoos, all sorts of things that might be tailored to an individual survivor's need. But those efforts don't stop traffickers.

The third category is stopping the traffickers themselves, and this is where we need to do more. I was talking to a trafficker not too long ago who was preparing to testify against his codefendants. During a break, he asked if the girls were in a shelter. I replied, "I'm not telling you where the girls are."

He laughed and said, "You all put so much energy into shelters and we are so done with them."

What he was saying is that he does not care about the names and faces of the people he has exploited. When we care for the people he has already discarded, it does not matter to him; he is done with them. We are not interfering with his business model. He will go out and find new people to exploit.

It became clear that we are getting better and better at caring for survivors—and we need to continue to expand our efforts there—but we are not getting better and better at stopping traffickers from harming more victims. We began to think about how we actually stop traffickers. What is exciting to me is that by moving upstream, we can begin to stop trafficking at its root. This is not true in other areas of need. For example, you can't stop an earthquake; you have to just care for the victims. In this case, however, it's a human being making a choice to use forced labor, so we can create change and stop trafficking if we stop that person from making that decision.

This requires law enforcement. Only law enforcement has the authority to stop traffickers. We have seen in many parts of the developing world that trafficking is exploding where the law is not being enforced. In developing countries, you are literally more likely to be struck by lightning than go to jail for openly owning slaves.

If there are no legal remedies on the ground, then trafficking flourishes. This is what the Human Trafficking Institute is taking on. We want to empower local criminal justice systems to take the protections that are written in laws, things that are passed by parliaments and congresses saying trafficking should not happen, and bring those in a meaningful way to the victims being exploited. And the way to do this is through law enforcement.

Let's think about it in a different context. Say there was a rash of burglaries in a community and someone was stealing things from homes. We could do a bunch of awareness-raising campaigns to let the community know there is an increase in burglaries. We could have campaigns to improve the lighting to make homes less vulnerable, and we could put better locks on the doors. We could do all these sorts of things on the awareness side. We could also care for the people who've been victims of the burglars. We could have support groups for them and insurance companies to help them replace the stolen goods. But first and foremost, we must stop the burglars.

This is what the world is crying out for. We need to stop this explosion of trafficking. The way it must be done is to stop the traffickers who are making an intentional choice to commit this crime.

We have learned there must be three things in place to be effective at enforcing the law. First, you've got to have the laws on the books.

We have seen tremendous progress in that area, so now every country in the world has laws against human trafficking. Second, you have to have the political will to enforce those laws. The police and prosecutors and judges have to want to enforce the law. We have also seen a transformation in political will as a result of applying some political pressure and providing economic incentives for countries to measurably reduce trafficking within their borders.

The challenge, however, is the third component, which is the capacity to enforce the law. For example, in places like India, 85 percent of the police receive virtually no training in criminal investigation, much less the ability to conduct a proactive human trafficking investigation and prosecution. Say we were thrown into a hospital and given scrubs, a mask, and a scalpel and told, "Okay, your family's livelihood depends on your ability to do cataract surgery on this line of patients out the door." At this point, it doesn't matter how incentivized we are, how smart we are, or how well-intentioned we are. We cannot do cataract surgery. This capacity gap is what we want to help countries fill.

We travel internationally to train prosecutors and judges on behalf of the Department of State or Homeland Security. We do this with the United Nations and others. We provide training in a fashion similar to residency in medical school. When someone becomes a physician they gain knowledge in medical school, but they also go through a residency program where they work under an experienced practitioner who helps them develop their skills. Skilled welders learn their trade and then do an apprenticeship; FBI agents go to the academy at Quantico and then get a field training officer. There is nothing like that in the developing world for criminal justice practitioners, and this is what we provide.

We join partner countries who are serious about decimating their trafficking. We first help them build specialized investigative and prosecutorial units and fast-track courts. These police officers' and prosecutors' sole focus becomes enforcing human trafficking laws. Then, second, we take those specialized units through an academy where they begin to gather the core knowledge they need to be effective. This might include how to do better case investigation, how to conduct a raid, how to do trauma-informed victim interviews, or how to build a successful trial strategy.

Once they go back to the unit and begin to work cases, they get the third component of training, which is a law enforcement mentor who has been successful at investigating and prosecuting human trafficking cases. This mentor will help them day in and day out to develop their skills and solve any case-related complications that arise, similar to a medical residency. Using those three components, we can begin to get that little bit of enforcement that brings about a large deterrent effect.

We know this works. My partner, Victor, and I were a part of the implementation and creation of this strategy with our colleagues at the Department of Justice. At that time six federal districts were selected for the first phase. In those six districts we employed the basic model of a specialized unit within law enforcement, helping give them a curriculum of training focused on best practices. We would fly to those cities and work cases with those prosecutors and agents in those six districts for two years. In those two years we saw an increase of 114 percent in the number of traffickers charged, while the other eighty-eight districts without this specialized support only saw a 12 percent increase. Amazingly, in those first two years, those six districts were responsible for over 50 percent of the nation's human trafficking convictions. That is, 50 to 56 percent of all the human trafficking convictions during those two years came from just those six districts. We now take this proven model and employ it in the developing world, where trafficking is exploding.

One thing everybody can do is to be informed about the dynamics of trafficking. When I first learned about trafficking, there was an incredible sense of being overwhelmed. I think it's hard for us to draw near to the pain of trafficking. Some of the people I visit with have a sense that what I'm telling them is just a drop in the ocean compared to the need. But I have a clear, tangible hope, because we have learned that trafficking is incredibly sensitive to risk. Traffickers make a decision to choose forced labor instead of voluntary labor because they know in many parts of the world they won't get in trouble for it. But as we equip law enforcement, we create a cost for traffickers. Once traffickers have to risk having their profits seized, losing their business, losing their freedom, and going to jail, we begin to see huge drops in the problem of trafficking.

To me this clear and tangible hope allows us to draw nearer to trafficking. We can think in innovative and creative ways about how to support those who are hurting from trafficking and how to move upstream to stop the crime at its source.

All the efforts focused on victim identification and victim care are essential, and those have to be part of a comprehensive approach to stop trafficking. But we are trying to advance the idea that in addition to that—not in place of it, but in addition to that—we also need to identify the traffickers. We need to find these individuals who are choosing to commit this crime. Good law enforcement is good at identifying criminals. If we can give them the political will and the resources to go out and do proactive investigations, both in sex trafficking and labor trafficking cases, we can rescue the victims and prosecute the traffickers. Rescuing the victims is essential, but identifying the traffickers and prosecuting them will end the cycle of exploitation.

Labor trafficking, based on numbers that come out of the International Labour Organization, seems to form a larger proportion of trafficking victims globally than sex trafficking, although sex trafficking seems to be more lucrative. The International Labour Organization has estimated that $150 billion in annual profits comes from trafficking. This is a staggering number. This is more than Apple, Samsung, Microsoft, BP, and Exxon combined. The vast majority of those profits are from sex trafficking.

Sex trafficking tends to be easier to find for a couple of reasons. First, the industry itself is illegal in many locations, so you often have police units, vice units, or the equivalent of vice units actively looking for that type of crime. Where you look, you will find. On the labor trafficking side, the work takes place in a legitimate industry. Hotels, restaurants, brick kilns, and rock quarries are legal operations in themselves. What is illegal is that they use forced labor. The challenge is that you may never see the laborer who is cleaning your hotel room or washing the dishes in the restaurant. Labor trafficking cases are definitely harder to identify, even though we know they are a larger proportion of the trafficking taking place globally.

Yet I am hopeful, because there is something we all can do to help put an end to trafficking. We all can get better informed and learn what is actually happening. If we prosecute traffickers, we start to see lots and lots of other traffickers abandon forced labor because it becomes too risky. By doing a little bit of enforcement, we not only help existing victims get the help they need, but we also prevent the future stream of victims from being exploited in the first place. We not only rescue current victims from the terrible trauma they are going through, but we wedge open the bottleneck that is choking out some other wonderful efforts that are already there to serve people and help them flourish and achieve their dreams.

IN SUMMARY

Those who enforce our laws need to be supported and equipped to handle the ever-changing injustices of our world. This includes law enforcement officers, attorneys, judges, and those who make and reform the laws. This does not necessarily mean we are off the hook as the church. We too are the people in places of power. As the church we have the power to care and support those who work in the justice system. As Gary Haugen states in his book *Terrify No More*, "Given all the power and resources that God has placed in the hands of humankind, I have yet to see any injustice of humankind that could not also be stopped by humankind."[12] We the church have the power of the Holy Spirit, Christ's very own resurrection power, the *imago Dei* empowering us to learn, to listen, to support, to create, to care. Haugen continues, "Even the bullies and tormentors of our world know that they never have enough power or force to withstand even a fraction of what people of goodwill could, by God's grace, bring to bear against them."[13]

BUILD A SAFETY FENCE: FENCEPOSTS

- Value and respect the role of law enforcement.
- Invite law enforcement representatives to your community events to build communication and trust.
- Find ways for your church to get involved in the greater community. This might be hosting a booth at a community event, volunteering at

an activity the city is putting on, or providing a meal for your local law enforcement station.

- Study Scripture with the theme of justice as your guide.
- As a church, consider financially supporting organizations that focus on the prosecution of traffickers.

6

PARTNERSHIP

CREATE LASTING CHANGE THROUGH COLLABORATION

Collaboration has to underpin every single thing that we do.

HELEN SWORN

Just as big as the human trafficking problem is, it takes an equal, if not greater size and effort of collaboration to tackle the problem.

JULIET OLIVER

COLLABORATION AND PARTNERSHIP ARE ESSENTIAL to ending human trafficking and modern slavery. Partnerships should be formed in all of the response areas: prevention, protection, prosecution, policy, and prayer. Strong partnerships are based on shared values, trust, teamwork, professional relationships, collaboration, and encouraging effective and lasting change.

There are three elements that characterize a healthy community collaboration network: value, trust, and density.[1] A survey tool available at Visible Network Labs that is used to evaluate task force effectiveness measures these three aspects of partnership. Here's a brief overview, which can help grow your church or nonprofit leadership's understanding and effectiveness. *Value* demonstrates the respect one member of the partnership holds for another. As you can imagine, if there's little value for another's contribution, there will be little trust. *Trust* grows when expectations are met. *Density* is measured by how many lines there are between partners and how strong those connections are. If the density score is low, the trust and value lines may be strong but few.

Now, imagine the safety fence illustration. Density has to do with the rails connecting your fenceposts to others'. If there are no rails, people will be pushed through the gaps between posts. With only a few posts, how many victims will continue to fall over the cliff? Another metaphor that helps us visualize this concept is a safety net. If there are only a few strands, the net will not catch vulnerable men, women, and children. But if there are multiple overlapping strands, the community will protect more vulnerable people.

Multidisciplinary teams and collaboration among groups are critical to meeting the demands of the complex issue of human trafficking. Key to collaboration is respect for various partners' expertise and resources. In William Wilberforce's efforts to end the transatlantic slave trade, he talked about overlapping networks. This idea can still inform how we build better and stronger collaborations today. It doesn't mean we all join the same circle and do everything the same way. We maintain our individual identities and figure out how we can work together to achieve a greater goal.

PRINCIPLES FOR EFFECTIVE PARTNERSHIP

Erin Albright, Former Director, New Hampshire Human Trafficking Collaborative Task Force[2]

The overlapping network analogy describes exactly what we have recognized to be necessary in the anti-trafficking world. We are recognizing that no one can do it alone. This term *collaboration* keeps popping up, and it is heavily dependent on building relationships with those in other fields. It is critical to making anti-human-trafficking work effective and being able to identify and support victims and hold perpetrators accountable.

There are three critical elements of building a task force. Leadership and structure are two of them, and culture is the third. We need strong leaders to be able to navigate all the twists, turns, and complications of bringing together these disparate parties who have similar and overlapping interests, but not the exact same interests. We need leaders and a strong team structure that supports what everybody is doing.

Culture is important. It is one of the softest and most overlooked elements of collaboration, but it can be the key to success. What culture means is setting up a tone within your group, setting up an atmosphere of collegiality, of honesty, and of open communication and trust. Important for me, especially in the trafficking world, is a culture of learning where you are constantly pushing yourselves to be better. Also crucial is a culture of transparency where everybody can come to the table and say, "I don't know the answer to this," or "I think this is a problem." Individuals need to feel safe and know that others will respond in a supportive way and not in a way that tries to tear them down or cast blame.

When it comes to collaboration, it is going to be messy. We might as well own it. If we acknowledge in advance that collaboration will be messy and complicated, we have perspective. I have worked on collaborative teams for over twelve years, and I have identified things I think are problematic with elements of culture. They are subtle things that people do not always have the language for, but they inevitably will happen in collaboration. Learning to flag these things in advance, for yourself and for teams you are part of, will help you address it.

Philosophical differences exist due to the very nature of multidisciplinary groups. Individuals have overlapping networks, but members are not all in the same circle. This means they each retain their own identities and their own roles. For instance, victim service providers often come from an underlying philosophy of empowerment or human rights. Law enforcement comes from a philosophy of criminal justice or rule of law. Grassroots folks involved in anti-trafficking work come from a community-organizing philosophy. If we enter collaborative spaces without acknowledging those different grounding philosophies, we miss a chance to mitigate tension down the road.

Groups that want to work together need to be prepared for a challenge of assumptions. It is easy to assume that your group is ready to respond to a trafficking case or hold an event or plan a ministry. But if that's not the truth, if you have just assumed that to be the case, you'll realize it quickly. Group readiness speaks to everybody. It helps everyone know why they are there, what their role is, and what other team members' roles are.

Role clarification is important because it mitigates conflict. Once you understand what that victim service provider is doing, you know what they can and cannot share with the group. This makes it easier for law enforcement to collaborate. Role clarification decreases frustration with others and helps avoid confusion for victims and survivors as well. It also helps identify gaps that may exist. We do not always have the right people in the room. This helps our strategic plan for filling any gaps.

These principles apply to any group of people working together for a common purpose. Respect and communication: these are the elements that will make our collaborative efforts stronger. We want to be stronger because we care about the people we serve.

THE IMPORTANCE OF NETWORKS

Helen Sworn, Founder of Chab Dai, Cambodia[3]

Chab Dai in the Cambodian language means "joining hands." That concept underpins everything we do as an organization. Whether we are doing prevention work, whether we are doing legal work, whether we are working within the coalition, whether we are doing research or advocacy, joining hands is how we do it.

I had been working for a number of years in a very cutthroat business world in the UK. My husband and I came to faith, and we had a sense that we wanted to move outside our comfort zone and go into some type of full-time Christian work. We thought we should study about this first. We went to seminary for three years, and while we were there we developed a heart to work with street kids and homeless youth. Southeast Asia opened up for us. We went for an internship and then moved at the beginning of 1999 with a small mission agency from the UK with our two children. Our daughter at the time was four, and our son was six months old. My husband set up a vocational training school in IT, and I went with my research and strategic planning background to help the organization and develop strategy for the next couple of years for the work he was doing.

One day I had a strong vision from God during a journey I took from Phnom Penh to the Thai-Cambodian border later in 1999. We had seen a lot of street kids and families going missing, and we could not work out what was happening. We did not have the language or even the term *human trafficking* then. We were just trying to figure out what was happening to these kids. I went on a challenging journey in a very old Russian prop plane that had chickens in the aisle, and I did not know whether we would get there safely. When we landed we hopped in a very old Land Cruiser and rode on horrendous roads the likes of which I had never seen before.

We got to the border area, and we started to see children. Many of them were being traded through the border in what we now understand to be human trafficking. Many of them were going into Thailand as beggars. I remember strikingly one four-year-old girl who had a six-month-old baby on her hip, which was the same age as my own kids at the time. She was totally responsible for this child. She did not know where her parents were or why they were gone. She had lost them on the streets in Bangkok somewhere. At that moment I knew this would be my life work. And that kept me in Cambodia for nineteen years.

At that time a lot of people were coming over from the United States, primarily Christians from churches, mission agencies, and other organizations who wanted to be part of the response. I started to see a human-trafficking-response environment that was chaotic. I compared it to a disaster situation when agencies from all over the world swarm into an area to try to address the needs.

It became apparent that the most critical need was coordination. If you do not have coordination among disaster agencies, then you'll have people who get seven meals a day in two shelters while others are starving to death with no shelter. Coordination and collaboration are critical in making sure you are serving the entire population.

I observed that everybody was coming with great intentions, but good intentions are not good enough. They are a great start, but we were seeing siloed responses. Organizations did not know the others existed. I started to see that we needed to do something about this. We needed to try to bring people together. In my naiveté I thought, *They are all going to want to work together, right? They are all Christians, aren't they? Why would they not want to work together?*

I started visiting with folks, saying, "Okay, we've got a problem that is way bigger than our individual organizations can address. What we need to do is get around the table together."

It took about eighteen months, even two years, to get organizations around that table. It was not easy. Two years later I finally got everybody together to look at the issues we were all addressing and the priorities we were all working on. I did basic baseline mapping to look at who was doing what and where. I included not just the Christian organizations around the table but also government and other groups. Then we looked at the gaps and the overlaps.

The result was striking to everybody. We had eleven organizations and about eight aftercare shelters, but there was no prevention work, no business development, and only a couple of groups doing intervention. It was easy to identify gaps when we came together.

I wanted to make sure we built a coalition that was helpful and useful. And we had certain nonnegotiable terms. The first was that everybody who wanted to be part of the coalition had to be legally registered with the Cambodian government. This is important. In many developing nations there is little rule of law or government oversight, so agencies go in and do what they like with little in the way of accountability. If you don't have accountability in terms of a government registration, I find that it permeates through your organization and ultimately through your practices. We saw organizations that refused to get government registration because they felt they were above the government morally. I could see that accountability was not something they held strongly to.

The second requirement was that they must have, or be willing to work with us to create, a child protection policy. Again, we were working beyond good intentions and at the baseline of doing no harm. Most of the organizations did not have any type of child protection policy or stakeholder protection policy. That was a non-negotiable for us at the beginning. Two simple principles that undergirded the work we were trying to do were accountability and safety for all beneficiaries.

I truly believe that one reason people are trafficked and exploited all over the world is that the criminals behind it are well networked. They don't need to like each other, and they don't need to be friends, but they need a common vision that enables them to focus on their networking. As responders, I find that we do not like to network. We are often much more interested in building empires, reputations, and egos, and we refuse to work with people because they have different theology or behave in ways that are upsetting and so on.

It comes right back down to a basic problem: If you have a network problem and you don't have a network solution, you're never going to be able to address human trafficking. Collaboration has to underpin every single thing we do. There is no one organization that has the competency to address this problem alone. There is no one sector that has all the competency. Not the NGO sector. Not academia. Not government. Collaboration is about working with community groups. It's about working with churches and individuals. In everything we build, we realize we have to get people to work in the area of their core competency and work together in a multidisciplinary way.

There's been a lot of academic study on social movements over generations. I believe that within the anti-trafficking sector in the last twenty years, we have seen the emergence of a movement. We know trafficking is a wicked problem both spiritually and academically. What we have to do is come together to build a movement for the long term. This is something people before us worked on for hundreds of years. Generations after us are going to be working on this. We need to build a movement. A movement will take our efforts beyond our lives and reach into the next generation.

We're trying to build what goes beyond us. Isn't that what a legacy is? We all want to leave a legacy, something that's not for us or our lifetime but what others can pick up and learn from. As we look at how this movement will mature, we need to look at the future. We need to look at the next generation of anti-trafficking practitioners, advocates, and academics and ask what they need from us. We have to have our vision and our focus on how we leave a legacy. What does that legacy look like?

BUILDING THE SAFETY FENCE: WHAT IT LOOKS LIKE

Bibiana MacLeod, Technical Adviser for Anti–Human Trafficking for Medical Ambassadors International, and Silvia Brynjolfson, Members of the World Evangelical Alliance Anti-Human-Trafficking Task Force and Co-coordinators of the Latin Anti-Human-Trafficking Forum

We are just at the beginning of building a Latin network against human trafficking. We are Christian women from Latin America living in Canada, and we are in our sixties. We are both experienced in many areas of ministry, yet anti–human trafficking was not one of them. Our common desire to obey God above anything else allowed us to come to him asking where to start getting involved, aware of our limitations with this issue. We both serve in ministries that sometimes overlap with one another, and this caused us to discover we share common values on leadership and ministry.

Silvia had started the process back in 2018, meeting in India with evangelical leaders who were focusing on human trafficking, and she continued to stay connected to this group through regular online meetings. We both attended an event with World Evangelical Alliance in February 2020, where we met more leaders in anti-human-trafficking work. This gathering had a global representation, yet it lacked connections with Latin America. That time revealed to all our ministries that a conversation about an anti-human-trafficking network in Latin America could get started. Thanks to others' perseverance in cultivating friendship with us, this seed started to germinate in us.

God had been orchestrating this new network, this new movement of which we were about to find ourselves a part, by promoting other friendships in our lives. Months earlier a key person had contacted Bibiana. She was serving in Cambodia, worked in Spain and in the Dominican Republic, and was exposed to the reality of victims exploited for sexual services in these countries. When we decided to explore what was happening in Latin America with anti-human-trafficking work, she helped us with our first contacts and even developed a Facebook page for us and helped with posts. From these original contacts, more and more people became connected with us.

During this time, we established our vision: first, to see Spanish-speaking abolitionists connecting with each other, aware that they are not alone and able to learn from each other, and second, to see the evangelical church involved at the level of their own opportunities and capacities, responding to the need in prevention, addressing and giving visibility to the issue, and, when possible, providing refuge, influencing policymakers, being salt and light in this specific problem.

In addition, Silvia is leading a prayer ministry for mothers who pray over their children in Latin America, and through this ministry she was in contact with evangelical alliances in many different countries. When she contacted them and invited them to join, or provide names of those people serving against human trafficking, more people came to the table. Our first meeting was in October 2020. Our agenda was simple. We asked what would they like to see happening with a new network of individuals and organizations working against human trafficking. After that meeting, the real networking began. We received calls asking if we knew someone in a particular country because there was a victim from that nation in another country and they needed a contact. More of these types of calls kept coming. The network started to work and to be valued.

During our online meetings people have the opportunity to introduce themselves and get to know and pray with each other. We met again in January and in March of 2021, incorporating new interested members. We take the time to interview those who want to join, finding out where they work and which field they focus on. Currently we have 189 individuals on our mailing list representing twenty-six organizations, twenty countries including Spain and Portugal, and many more local churches. Other faith-based organizations also participate in the network. God is using every piece of experience, relationships, ministry, skills, and time to form an organic movement that lives beyond each of its parts.

IN SUMMARY: THE PITHARI

In ancient Crete, the palace kitchens had huge jars called *pithari*—some were so huge a person could stand up inside. These jars were used to take oil and grain down the steep stairs into the kitchen. There were no cranes at this time to carry heavy loads, so the ancient Minoans designed the *pithari* so that many handles covered the entire surface: top, sides, and even close to the bottom. This design ensured that everyone could find a handle and help carry the load (see figure 4).

Figure 4. Ancient Manoan kitchen jar

This image is useful to the church today as we begin to imagine our role in engaging and fighting the enormous and overwhelming issue of global human trafficking. No one church or organization can do everything. We just need to find our handle. The only way we will end human trafficking and modern slavery is by working together as faith communities, working together with agencies and organizations outside of the church, and through real and effective collaboration.

BUILD A SAFETY FENCE: FENCEPOSTS

- In partnership, the elements of value, trust, and density move fenceposts closer together, deepen foundations, and strengthen the overall safety fence.
- Value means growing in respect and understanding of the expertise and resources of your collaborators.
- Trust means having oversight and intentional follow-up to ensure that as a church you do what you say you are going to do. Keep your word in the public and private sectors.

- Density means not playing favorites or respecting only one group. Invest in relationships that represent a diverse perspective on issues relating to human trafficking. Link your fenceposts to wide, diverse, and overlapping networks.

7

POLICY

CHURCHES AND NONPROFITS

And this is my prayer: that your love may abound more and more in knowledge and depth of insight, so that you may be able to discern what is best and may be pure and blameless for the day of Christ, filled with the fruit of righteousness that comes through Jesus Christ—to the glory and praise of God.

PHILIPPIANS 1:9-10

We are now at the fifth P—policy. Policies may seem dry and boring, but they serve a critical purpose. They create process, which helps develop patterns of ethical best practices. Ethical practices build trust in our communities and give us language to operationalize our value for human dignity. Policies also provide concrete tools to measure our effectiveness in reaching goals, internally as well as in the community. Just as we used the Ps as the framework for this book, let's use them to identify the policies a church or nonprofit organization needs to have in place. Policies are clear and transparent, designed to protect the vulnerable as well as church leaders, church members, and staff. When we talk about policy we are talking about best practices, ethical guidelines that are written down and shared with leadership and volunteers. Everyone agrees to follow and be accountable to these guidelines.

What we know from those serving in pastoral leadership roles, and from those who volunteer in churches in addition to working in their professional careers, is that leaders are often functioning at maximum capacity. Our hope for this book is not to overwhelm. Not every church has to have a separate ministry addressing human trafficking, but in providing information and language around the problem, we hope to help leaders see strategic ways their church may already be addressing this problem. Policies that create opportunities for review will build dynamic change that may eliminate time-consuming or expensive programs in order to pour into another ministry that is more effective. Whatever course of action you take, we believe having policies for your church, ministry, or organization is important to protect your central mission to be light and salt, drawing people to Christ.

THE P OF PREVENTION

We start with prevention because we believe God's plan is for all of creation to experience physical and mental health. Specific to human trafficking, we believe that each church needs a written requirement that staff and volunteers undergo basic human trafficking training. This ensures two things. First, your church will reduce its vulnerability to unscrupulous organizations that trade on sensational stories because everyone will be trained and know what questions to ask. Second, your staff will know when something doesn't seem right and can either refer or report a potential situation of exploitation and avoid taking action that may be harmful to the victim, the staff or volunteer, and the church.

Wise leaders intentionally build in value for prevention, or, as grandmothers say, "An ounce of prevention is worth a pound of cure." Valuing prevention saves resources, including money, people, and goodwill in the community. To maintain this approach, plan an annual ministry audit that purposely reviews ministries for overlooked value. In the mission to ensure justice for those being crushed, some ministries can seem less exciting and be disregarded, such as snacks delivered once a week for a local afterschool program. But a church that desires to keep children safe and knows students are alone for hours after school is to be commended; this snack ministry is a prevention strategy. A church we know of in Florida did a fundraising campaign for an afterschool program called "Popsicles Prevent Pregnancy" in response to a situation in their community in which a ten-year-old girl had become pregnant. This young girl had regularly gone home to an empty apartment because her mother worked full time, and she was raped by another resident of the apartment complex. An afterschool snack program may have prevented this young girl from being so vulnerable.

Part of a ministry audit focused on prevention involves knowing that early abuse is often a part of a victim's history. Therefore it's important to review your child protection policy. No one is above the law. Many trafficking victims are first exploited by someone they know, and that includes abuse by someone in their church. Your church insurance company will have guidelines on protecting children, but one thing you can do is simply ensure that two adults are always present when ministering to children. For example, youth pastors are not allowed to give a teen a solo ride home, male or female.

Prevention is also an opportunity to consider stewardship and develop procurement policies that do not drive demand for cheap products and services. Consider creating a policy focused on ethically sourced products. Does your church or organization purchase coffee or chocolate? Does it create merchandise with its logo on it? Be sure to be thorough when investigating and learning what products your church or organization consumes and where these products originate. Best practice is to promote a procurement policy that is based on supply chain review. Buy as directly sourced or fairly traded as possible. There are ethically sourced coffee, chocolate, cotton T-shirts, and bags out there. We own them; we buy them. The church can too. We cannot exploit people who make our goods and then turn around and send money through mission organizations back to the poor people in that country.

THE P OF PROTECTION

The goal of policies around protection is to value people over programs and to provide support and services for restoration and healthy reintegration in society. Protecting the dignity of victims and survivors is an ethical responsibility with clearly defined best practices and standards that are survivor-informed. Policies that are often overlooked in churches concern media as well as engagement with survivors who may be in different stages of their healing journey.

Media and images. It is important for churches and organizations to have a policy about images and how those images are used. There are laws that regulate the posting of images of children regardless of whether they are children of regular attendees or members. There should already be a policy in your church or organization requiring permission from the child's parent to share any image of a minor. What we are encouraging goes beyond this. A best practice related to human trafficking is that all images and communications should protect the dignity and worth of victims and be truthful. Too often media images sensationalize human trafficking, depicting victims in chains or duct tape over a child's mouth, like something from an overdramatic Hollywood movie. Rarely does a victim of human trafficking need to be rescued from actual chains. Images like these detract from the actual problem and distort the conversation. They can cause us to look for the wrong signs of human trafficking and miss the cases right in front of our eyes. There are real human beings caught up in the crime of human trafficking. Every image should honor both the person in the image and those the image represents. Even if you visit a country that does not protect the image of a child, as the church, we should hold the same standard for children from that country that we have for our children.

A survivor-informed media policy ensures that our media use no images involving chains or other sensationalized situations. Media must never show children or adults in vulnerable positions, in pain, or being abused. Our media policy must protect the identity and dignity of everyone. A way to begin might be to ask some clarifying questions such as, "Is the way we are presenting this topic honoring survivors?" Survivor-informed leadership is a best practice, and resources are available to assist in evaluating your media campaigns.

Ask a survivor what they think before posting a message on social media or sharing certain images or using a packaged video clip during a service or event. This is an extremely helpful practice. Survivors consistently say that what upsets them most is the use of sensationalized images because survivors know if others are taught to only look for the worst, they will miss the victim right in front of them. Practitioners across the globe in the anti-human-trafficking movement have learned to consult survivors as much as possible. They are the true experts.

Also, be sure you have permission to use an image. We need to respect the dignity of all, and we need to protect our witness to a watching world. Messaging in our media should be empowering. For example, consider using the word *restore* over *rescue* or *save*. *Restore* is more accurate and more empowering.

Community engagement. As noted earlier, a policy that provides for each staff member or volunteer to have a basic overview of human trafficking will ensure that everyone has a clearer lens for viewing the people they encounter, whether they're providing meal packages, teaching a vacation Bible school class, tutoring in an afterschool program, or ushering on Sunday morning. By incorporating human trafficking awareness and training across programs, ministries, and missions, the local church is equipped to be eyes and ears identifying, reporting, and referring no matter where you are in the world or in your local community. The more educated you and your congregation are about human trafficking, the more readily you will see it when in the field ministering. It's similar to those times when you buy a new make and model of vehicle, and suddenly you start seeing that same vehicle everywhere—awareness makes you notice.

Likewise, once educated, people more often identify possible exploitation. Education gives us eyes to see what we did not see before. Basic training must also include a plan for what to do when you suspect trafficking. Your plan should include information on who to notify and where to report. If your church or organization is working internationally, we recommend researching how to report in the countries you visit or serve. Review the countries where your church supports missions. Study the human trafficking trends there and learn the local resources and hotline numbers. Youth groups can do country studies as part of their global mission projects. Mission teams can review the annual *Trafficking in Persons Report* specific to the country they will be visiting before they travel. No matter where you are, you can always report to your own embassy, so make sure to have that number with you. If in the United States, you can report to local law enforcement and the National Human Trafficking Hotline number, 888-373-7888. When you see signs of something that looks suspicious, report it; do not confront it.

Victim and survivor support policies. It's important for the policies in our churches to emphasize that our interactions and activities should not be transactional. When someone is in great need, we can demonstrate God's love with no expectation of gratitude or other return on our investment. While our church mission may be rooted in proclaiming the gospel, let us be mindful that when helping others, we simply help others with no expectation that they say thank you, and we do not assume that they desire to come to Christ or join the church. We have seen that when people in survival mode are provided with the basic necessities of life, some will say whatever they think you want to hear if it assures them they have a place to sleep or food in their stomachs. Holding expectations of how someone should respond when you offer assistance is transactional; it is not transformational. Recognize when a survivor may feel obligated even when that is not your intention or when a volunteer misrepresents your organization's genuine "no strings attached" service.

Training on being trauma-informed and integrating this in regular ministry discipleship lessons can help you avoid this problem. We have seen organizations ask survivors to sign "committed my life to Jesus" cards in order to receive services. Don't leverage what you have to give so they do what you want them to do. They know what you want them to do. They know what to say. They're survivors. They have done what they needed to in order to survive. If they need to sign a card, they will. Please consider the ethics of this and always honor the *imago Dei* in each person.

At a recent Vanguard University Ensure Justice annual conference, survivor advocate Bella Hounakey emphasized the immense value of church support when she spoke to attendees: "The shame, the guilt, the regret that you carry as a survivor, it follows you. It's like being hunted by your own shadow. The more you're around a community that reminds you of the goodness that God has in you, [the more] you start identifying with the ways that you're being perceived by this community of people.

"I thought I had depleted my community of support. They were a group of people, believers, who were committed to the entire me. . . . They took the time to build trust with me, they took the time to understand me, and they didn't force anything. So, I knew that for the first time in my life, somebody really just wanted to help me without asking anything in return. It took a really long time for me to conceptualize that, to understand that this group of people wanted to give me a ride after school at 6:00 p.m. or 5:00 p.m. without asking anything in return. Those were ways that they helped. They were present, consistently.

"Now when the church steps in, I know that for the trafficker to have access to me again, they have to go through this community of people, which was my church, in order to get to me. That alone gave me shelter. Not physical shelter. It gave me an emotional shelter."

Protecting children in your community and elsewhere. Whether you are in the United States or overseas, you must follow the same policies for protecting children from sexual abuse. People are often background-checked, but a background check is not really enough. The church must have policies that are enforced. No child is to be left alone with a single adult. When you go to another country where they don't have the same laws, you still follow the same policies; you still follow best practices to protect children. For example, it is unethical for an organization that cannot post pictures of child victims in the United States to post pictures of child victims from another country.

THE P OF PROSECUTION

Policies around prosecution are based on legal requirements. It is strongly suggested that churches not engage in work that involves investigation or rescue. That is the responsibility of our law enforcement agencies. Well-intentioned efforts may put the local church at risk for lawsuits and place church members and victims in harm's way.

THE P OF PARTNERSHIP

Policies on partnership should recognize roles and clarify commitments. Unmet expectations are the most common cause of broken relationships, personally and in the community. For instance, policies clarify things such as: Can a member of a local church speak for the leadership and commit facilities to a local task force for an event? How are resource commitments made? Who decides how long to serve and how much to give? And so on.

Partnerships that serve victims of human trafficking must also have strong confidentiality agreements. If a church partners with an organization that then offers a victim's story to the media, even though the church was not responsible, the church's reputation will suffer. Consequently, it is important to establish that other partners have the same standards as your church.

Annual policy reviews can include reviewing your list of human trafficking partnerships. If the person who supported a certain ministry is no longer available, it is better for community relationships to let the other party know that the resource (people and time are resources) is no longer available.

THE P OF POLICY

Policy also requires a policy. It is important to have policies written down and available for everyone to review. Take time to review policies once a year to make sure you are compliant and to evaluate the effectiveness of each. Every year policies will improve and get stronger based on what you have learned and experienced. An annual review refines and evaluates effectiveness and ensures policies are being used. Every department should have a binder or computer folder with policies available for all to read and review. Make sure to include all volunteers when training on policies.

BUILD A SAFETY FENCE: FENCEPOSTS

- Take time to educate your leadership team on the issue of human trafficking and begin the process of prayerfully thinking through your specific church or organizational policies.

- Create a plan to implement the policies. Policies should be written down with accountability built in.
- Consult a survivor during the policy creation and review process if possible.
- Be intentional about education: Plan to have at least one sermon on the subject of human trafficking every year. Include the root cause, greed. The Bible says the love of money is the root of all kinds of evil (1 Timothy 6:10). Remember it is a supply-and-demand issue, and we all are consumers demanding something.
- Review the year's efforts in anti–human trafficking to be sure that the focus has been balanced between sex and labor trafficking.
- Review the countries where your church supports missions. Study the human trafficking trends there; learn the local resources and hotline numbers before making trips. Ask missionaries what their involvement is in local anti-human-trafficking efforts.

8

PRAYER

STAND FIRM

For our struggle is not against flesh and blood, but against the rulers, against the authorities, against the powers of this dark world and against the spiritual forces of evil in the heavenly realms.

EPHESIANS 6:12

It is not a mental leap to understand the truth of the verse above when one is learning the magnitude and pervasiveness of human trafficking. Slavery, both historically and presently, is evil. The dehumanization of another human being is a dark stain on humanity. Suspending recognition of the *imago Dei* in another person, treating them as a commodity to be bought and sold, is clearly not how God created us to live. The sinfulness of human trafficking does not need to be explained or unpacked. It is clear. It is not from God but the evil one.

It is likely that as we learn what is ours to do in response to the global problem of modern-day slavery, we will become overwhelmed. It is overwhelming. It is dark. The stories we encounter will be horrific, and the experiences survivors have endured will break your heart. We might know this on an intellectual level, but at some point (or at many points) it will rock our soul to the core. This is not easy work. It is going to get difficult and messy, and we will experience tears and anger. Prayer, both individual and corporate, is essential in the fight against human trafficking. The expression "fight against human trafficking" is not just an expression; it is truth. This is a fight. There is a battle being waged, and although we might not see the spiritual battle around us, we do see the physical consequences of the battle when we hear stories, meet survivors, and begin to plan strategically to engage in the fight.

We need to first recognize it is a battle. This is more than a battle of flesh and blood—although our practical call is to care for the flesh and blood of other people, it is essential that we also engage the spiritual side of this battle through prayer. Knowing we are in a battle, we must prepare for warfare. We cannot be lazy, we cannot cut corners, we must be in shape, we must be strategic, and we must act.

> Therefore put on the full armor of God, so that when the day of evil comes, you may be able to stand your ground, and after you have done everything, to stand. Stand firm then, with the belt of truth buckled around your waist, with the breastplate of righteousness in place, and with your feet fitted with the readiness that comes from the gospel of peace. In addition to all this, take up the shield of faith, with which you can extinguish all the flaming arrows of the evil one. Take the helmet of salvation and the sword of the Spirit, which is the word of God.
>
> And pray in the Spirit on all occasions with all kinds of prayers and requests. With this in mind, be alert and always keep on praying for all the Lord's people. (Ephesians 6:13-18)

Notice that this passage of Ephesians does not direct us into physical battle. Instead it reminds us that we are to stand our ground, and in order to do so we must have the right protective armor. God is the one who is ahead taking charge. We are to stand firm with appropriate armor, with a mind that is alert, and we are to pray. We battle with the spiritual weapon of the Word of God, and we battle when we pray in the Spirit.

Prayer often brings our hands up in praise and lowers us to our knees in desperation. Prayer reminds us we are not God. Prayer is humbling. It does not always bring about images of superheroes who defeat bad guys and rescue damsels in distress. But this does not mean we dismiss the power of prayer and its foundational essentialness. There is absolutely no victory against the evil of human trafficking without prayer. No laws, no governments, no intervention strategy, no unique logo, no passionate speech, no documentary will ever defeat the evil manifestation of human trafficking without prayer being our foundation. This unique and powerful work can be done only through God's people. Only human beings created in the image of God, indwelt with the supernatural power of the Holy Spirit in prayer, can join God's heavenly army and once and for all put an end to human trafficking. When the church does what only the church can do, heaven will be ushered in in miraculous ways on earth and justice will be restored.

As Oswald Chambers says, "Prayer does not fit us for the greater works; prayer *is* the greater work."[1]

Despite this chapter on prayer coming at the end of this book, we believe prayer is not an afterthought but the most important work the church can undertake. Prayer is the lane the church is most equipped to be in. It is so natural for the church and its members to pray that sometimes we overlook its essential work and power. For some people, praying individually or corporately might not look or feel exciting. We don't often get to see immediate results after praying, and sometimes we don't see the results of our prayers in our lifetime. Again, Chambers beautifully reminds us that "it is the labouring saint who makes the conceptions of his Master possible. You labour at prayer and results happen all the time from His standpoint. What an astonishment it will be to find, when the veil is lifted, the souls that have been reaped by you, simply because you had been in the habit of taking your orders from Jesus Christ."[2]

Our calling to pray is true of both the local church and the church universal. The church is uniquely created to pray and is strategically positioned for prayer in the battle against evil. The church can be found across the world in neighborhoods, government agencies, places of work, mission fields, businesses, schools, and our own homes. We have enough bodies strategically positioned that we need to be adequately equipped and willing to engage courageously.

Our prayer is that this book would be used to equip you and the greater church to see and better understand the magnitude of the problem of human trafficking and help guide you and your church in discovering a thoughtful and effective response. We may not have the privilege of seeing the answers to our prayers, but we trust that when we obey and do our part, we join the saints who have gone before us in helping to usher in heaven on earth. We pray in confidence, knowing the battle is already won in the resurrection and redemptive work of Jesus Christ, and we are excited for you to join us.

> Devote yourselves to prayer, being watchful and thankful. (Colossians 4:10)

Take prayer seriously and plan for it. If your church doesn't already have a prayer team, consider designating a group of people who are entirely committed to praying for your church and its mission weekly. Make sure to educate them on the issue of human trafficking so they can incorporate prayer on this matter. Consider physically going out to your community with the sole purpose of looking and listening for where God leads. Pray as you walk the blocks around your church building, or go into a specific neighborhood for the sole purpose of praying. During this time your team is not planning, nor are they actively participating in service. You and your prayer team are simply asking God to meet you there and then listening. He might reveal something or he might not. But the practice of going out in your community, rural or urban, outside your church building, and praying for your community is a very powerful anti-trafficking move. Ask God for eyes to see your community the way he sees it. Later, debrief as a team to discern what if anything was revealed. Consider doing this many times before acting. Be patient in prayer and wait for God to act first. Then follow. Consider joining other churches in prayer. One way to do this is to join the Faith Alliance Against Slavery and Trafficking, which hosts an annual Pray for Freedom event in January (see faastinternational.org/take-action/freedom-sunday). You can also plan a prayer focus on the United Nations World Day Against Trafficking in Human Beings every July 30.

Another way to draw your church community together in prayer around the problem of human trafficking is to pray through the Ps we have mentioned throughout this book: prevention, protection, prosecution, partnership, and policy. Below we have included prayers around the Ps you can use or model your own around these themes.

THE P OF PREVENTION

Lord, we come to you humbly, knowing we can effectively do nothing without you going before us, leading us, clearing a path before us. We want to listen and obey wherever you lead in ending human trafficking. We want to do our part to prevent this evil from even beginning in the first place. We pray for the people and institutions who are in positions of prevention. We lift up teachers, schools, community centers, our local churches, our local YMCAs and Boys and Girls Clubs, homeless shelters, and food banks. We pray for creativity and an abundance of resources as they serve our children and those vulnerable in our community. In Jesus' name, Amen.

THE P OF PROTECTION

Lord, we lift up our own church community and others in our local area. We pray for humility, wisdom, creativity, and strength as we do our part to protect the most vulnerable in our community. We pray for eyes to see those hurting in our own congregations and those hurting just outside our walls in our community. Help us see the need and give us empathy to act in loving and healing ways.

We pray for single mothers and fathers struggling to care for their children. We lift to you families displaced by conflict and violence. We pray for school counselors, coaches, and other adults in positions of listening and learning about the risks of the minors they serve. Give them insight, compassion, and wisdom to know what to do to protect children from being exploited or hurt. We lift up parents and grandparents and other guardians in our congregations and in our greater community. We pray for their bonds of love to be strengthened. We pray for insight, wisdom, and strength as they listen and care for the children and young adults they have influence over. We pray we would be a church that is not corrupted by greed and the world's values. We pray we would be good stewards who wisely support leaders who ensure fair wages to those who produce the goods and services we use. In Jesus' name, Amen.

THE P OF PROSECUTION

Lord, we lift up everyone who interacts with victims of human trafficking. We pray for social workers, advocates, and volunteers who are directly in contact with victims. Give them insight and wisdom, and equip them with all the resources they need to care for and support victims throughout their healing process. We pray for the law enforcement and health-care workers who come into contact with victims or are working on cases on their behalf. Bless them with understanding and wisdom. We lift up all victims of human trafficking. Hear their cries, comfort them, and restore them to full healing the way only you can.

Clear the path for justice. Guide the court system and provide the evidence necessary for building strong legal cases so justice will be served on behalf of victims. We pray for the attorneys and judges involved in these cases. Give them understanding and wisdom as they listen and execute justice in the courts. We pray for our entire judicial system. We pray for stronger laws that serve the most vulnerable in our communities. We pray for justice to be served in compassionate and healing ways for victims. In Jesus' name, Amen.

THE P OF PARTNERSHIP

Lord, we pray for the strengthening of partnerships across private and public sectors. We pray for understanding, respect, and unity among agencies, organizations, churches, law enforcement groups—anyone who is in a position of influence and serves on behalf of the most vulnerable to trafficking in our communities. We pray for humility, a spirit of respect, and a posture of learning from one another. In Jesus' name, Amen.

THE P OF POLICY

Lord, we pray for strong laws both locally and globally, laws that will serve and protect the most vulnerable in our communities. We pray for fair and just laws. We pray for our local, state, and national leaders. Guide their decisions. Grant them wisdom and courage to serve the neediest in our communities and in the greater world. We pray for the Trafficking Victims Protection Act. We pray that with each passing year it will become stronger, more robust, and sufficiently resourced to serve victims and provide clarity for national leaders. We pray for the United Nations and all international agencies that are working on behalf of trafficking victims and working to prevent others from falling victim. We pray for unity, for wisdom, for collaboration, for courage to continue to do the right thing in serving the most needy. In Jesus' name, Amen.

CONFESSION

> If my people, who are called by my name, will humble themselves and pray and seek my face and turn from their wicked ways, then I will hear from heaven, and I will forgive their sin and will heal their land. (2 Chronicles 7:14)

Historically, the church has been complicit in the enslavement of other human beings. The Church of England's missionary arm, the Society for the Propagation of the Gospel in Foreign Parts, owned the Codrington plantation in Barbados and even branded the slaves who worked there with the word "society" on their chests. They were so blinded by this sin that they documented in detail the business of their sugar plantation and the brutality of the slave trade, of which they were actively and knowingly a part.[3]

This was not the only time the church has been blinded by sin and added tremendous harm to the anti-slavery movement. It was not the only time people who claimed to be followers of Jesus Christ abused or ignored the pleas of the poor, the widow, the orphan, those in prison, or the enslaved. The truth is, the church—and anyone who claims Jesus as Lord and Savior—has much to confess.

When we pray, let's begin with confession: confession of the church's historical blindness to slavery and its complicity in it, as well as confession of not seeing the vulnerable in our own communities.

> Woe to him who builds his palace by unrighteousness,
> his upper rooms by injustice,
> making his countrymen work for nothing,
> not paying them for their labor. (Jeremiah 22:13)

Let's confess our blindness to the harmful effects of and tolerant attitude toward pornography and other sexual exploitations in our society. Let's confess the ways our consumer culture demands cheap goods and services at the expense of others' dignity and humanity. As we begin to corporately confess, we may uncover personal or individual sins that we also need to confess. We believe that as you and your church humbly begin to confess, you will be better positioned to fight against human trafficking in your community.

> For though we live in the world, we do not wage war as the world does. The weapons we fight with are not the weapons of the world. On the contrary, they have divine power to demolish strongholds. (2 Corinthians 10:3-4)

Evil cannot thrive where God's people humble themselves, confess their sins, take time to listen to God, and obey. There is tremendous power when the church obeys God's directives to care for orphans, widows, those in prison, the poor, the hungry, the most vulnerable in our communities. When we obey God, evil flees.

Just as the church has been complicit in slavery, so it is has also led the abolitionist movement. At the same time the Church of England owned slave-labored sugar plantations, the Quakers, a small Christian community in Britain, came out publicly against slavery, and many were persecuted for this belief. They believed in the *imago Dei*, what they referred to as the "inner light," in all people regardless of race or class. They worked tirelessly and creatively to get the attention of the British elite and were often ignored, dismissed, or even thrown into prison. They were relentless and uncompromising, and eventually the hearts and minds of a few British leaders were changed, clear vision of the evil of slavery was now understood, and the battle of ending of the transatlantic slave trade was officially waged.

Likewise, just as the church in the United States was part of the problem of slavery, so it was also a crucial part of the abolitionist movement and the Underground Railroad system in which slaves were brought to freedom. The church is a powerful force when it seeks the Lord first. In order to operate effectively and in love, we must submit and commit ourselves to the Lord our God first and foremost.

> Follow justice and justice alone, so that you may live and possess the land the LORD your God is giving you. (Deuteronomy 16:20)

Read and study Joshua. See how seeking God first in prayer before doing anything is essential in battle. Don't do it alone. Don't go ahead of God. Look at the rhythms of Jesus' own life, when he spent days and nights in prayer before entering the public arena. Go before the feet of God and seek him. Confess and turn from sin. Pray. Listen. Put on the armor of God. In the power of Jesus' name, do not fear but go out and obey.

Blessed are those whose help is the God of Jacob,
whose hope is in the LORD their God.

He is the Maker of heaven and earth,
the sea, and everything in them—
he remains faithful forever.
He upholds the cause of the oppressed
and gives food to the hungry.
The LORD sets prisoners free,
the LORD gives sight to the blind,
the LORD lifts up those who are bowed down,
the LORD loves the righteous.
The LORD watches over the foreigner
and sustains the fatherless and the widow,
but he frustrates the ways of the wicked.

The LORD reigns forever,
your God, O Zion, for all generations. (Psalm 146:5-10)

There is an ebb and flow in anti-trafficking work. We may begin with confidence and an emboldened energy as we undertake justice work. This may be followed by fatigue, tears, and wondering if you are making a difference. You might find yourself battling indifference or confusion. No matter where you find yourself in this fight, continually be grounded in prayer. Lead with prayer always, and when you find yourself depleted, as you most likely will, hold on to this truth: "In the same way, the Spirit helps us in our weakness. We do not know what we ought to pray for, but the Spirit himself intercedes for us through wordless groans. And he who searches our hearts knows the mind of the Spirit, because the Spirit intercedes for God's people in accordance with the will of God" (Romans 8:26-27). If you continue to lead with prayer and be grounded in prayer, the Spirit himself will intercede when words fail.

Church, stand firm,

> with the belt of truth buckled around your waist, with the breastplate of righteousness in place, and with your feet fitted with the readiness that comes from the gospel of peace. In addition to all of this, take up your shield of faith,

with which you can extinguish all the flaming arrows of the evil one. Take the helmet of salvation and the sword of the Spirit, which is the word of God.

And pray in the Spirit on all occasions with all kinds of prayers and requests. With this in mind be alert and always keep on praying for the all the Lord's people. (Ephesians 6:14-18)

Lord, we commit this book and its contents to you now. Use it as you will to equip and empower your people to go out and serve the most vulnerable in our communities. Guide and protect them as they step out in obedience. Bless them with wisdom and creativity as they join you in the fight against human trafficking. Pour out your unfailing love on and through them as they step out to be salt and light to a hurting world. We thank you and praise you for your goodness and love. We give you all of ourselves and our work to use for your good purposes. In Jesus' name, Amen.

Appendix A

COMMON ABBREVIATIONS AND GLOSSARY

CSAM	child sexual abuse material
SG-CSAM	self-generated child sexual abuse material
CSEC	commercial sexual exploitation of children
DHS	US Department of Homeland Security
DOJ	US Department of Justice
HHS	US Department of Health and Human Services
ICAC	Internet Crimes Against Children
ICE	US Immigration and Customs Enforcement
NGO	nongovernmental organization
NHTRC	National Human Trafficking Resource Center
OAS	Organization of American States
ORR	Office of Refugee Resettlement
OVC	Department of Justice Office of Victims of Crimes
PITF	President's Interagency Task Force to Monitor and Combat Human Trafficking
three Ps or 3Ps	protection, prevention, prosecution
TIP Report	*Trafficking in Persons Report*
TVPA	Trafficking Victims Protection Act
UNODC	United Nations Office on Drugs and Crime
USCIS	US Citizenship and Immigration Services

GLOSSARY[1]

child soldiers—Involves the unlawful recruitment or use of children through force, fraud, or coercion as combatants, or for labor or sexual exploitation by armed forces. Perpetrators may be government forces, paramilitary organizations, or rebel groups. Some children are made to work as porters, cooks, guards, servants, messengers, or spies. Young girls can be forced to marry or have sex with male combatants.

child trafficking—Forms of child trafficking include trafficking for purposes of sexual exploitation, labor trafficking, removal of organs, illicit international adoption, trafficking for early marriage, recruitment as child soldiers, use in begging, and recruitment of athletes.

coercion—Under the TVPA, coercion is defined as (1) threats of serious harm or physical restraint; (2) any scheme, plan, or pattern intended to cause a person to believe that failure to perform an act would result in serious harm to or physical restraint against any person; or (3) the abuse or threatened abuse of the legal process.

commercial sex act—Under the TVPA, commercial sex act means any sex act on account of which anything of value is given to or received by any person.

commercial sexual exploitation of children (CSEC)—In 1996, the World Congress Against Commercial Sexual Exploitation of Children defined CSEC as sexual abuse of a child by an adult and remuneration in cash or kind to the child or a third person. The child is treated as a sexual object and a commercial object. CSEC includes the prostitution of children, child pornography, child sex tourism, and other forms of transactional sex where a child engages in sexual activities to have key needs fulfilled, such as food, shelter, or access to education. It includes forms of transactional sex where the sexual abuse of children is not stopped or reported by household members due to benefits derived by the household from the perpetrator.

Convention Against Transnational Organized Crime (a.k.a. the Palermo Convention)—UN-sponsored multilateral treaty adopted in 2000 contains the Protocol to Prevent, Suppress and Punish Trafficking in Persons, Especially Women and Children. The convention and the protocol fall under the jurisdiction of the United Nations Office on Drugs and Crime (UNODC).

debt bondage—Under the TVPA, debt bondage means the status or condition of a debtor arising from a pledge by the debtor of his or her personal services or of those of a person under his or her control as a security for debt, if the value of those services as reasonably assessed is not applied toward the liquidation of the debt or the length and nature of those services are not respectively limited and defined.

demand-side approach to combating sex trafficking—This approach focuses on enhancing and encouraging the enforcement of penalties against those who buy commercial sex.

Department of Health and Human Services HHS Certification—Issued by the US Department of Health and Human Services (HHS) Office of Refugee Resettlement (ORR), certification allows adult victims of trafficking who are not US citizens or lawful permanent residents to be eligible to receive benefits and services under any federal or state program or activity to the same extent as a refugee. To receive certification, a person who is eighteen years of age or older must be a victim of a severe form of trafficking, be willing to assist in every reasonable way in the investigation and prosecution of severe forms of trafficking or be unable to cooperate due to physical or psychological trauma, and have made a bona fide application for a T visa that has not been denied, or have received Continued Presence from the Department of Homeland Security (DHS) in order to contribute to the prosecution of traffickers in person. Foreign child victims of trafficking (under the age of eighteen) do not need to be certified to receive benefits and services.

Department of Justice Civil Rights Division—In addition to enforcing existing laws against trafficking, the Civil Rights Division is responsible for investigating cases of trafficking and prosecuting traffickers.

Department of Justice Office of Victims of Crimes (OVC)—Provides funds to programs and organizations that assist victims of trafficking.

Department of State's Office to Monitor and Combat Trafficking in Persons (TIP Office)—Created by the TVPA of 2000, this office partners with foreign governments and civil society to develop and implement effective strategies for confronting modern-day slavery. The office has responsibility for bilateral and multilateral diplomacy, targeted foreign assistance, and public engagement on trafficking in persons.

domestic trafficking—Refers to the trafficking of US citizens within the United States.

Executive Order Strengthening Protections in Federal Contracts (2012)—Prohibits federal contractors, subcontractors, and their employees from engaging in certain trafficking-related practices, such as conducting misleading or fraudulent recruitment practices, charging employees recruitment fees, and destroying or confiscating an employee's identity documents, such as a passport or a driver's license. It also requires that for work exceeding $500,000 that is performed abroad, federal contractors and subcontractors must maintain compliance plans appropriate for the nature and scope of the activities performed. Furthermore, it establishes a process to identify industries and sectors that have a history of human trafficking, to enhance compliance on domestic contracts, and augment training and heighten agencies' ability to detect and address trafficking violations.

human smuggling—The facilitation, transportation, attempted transportation, or illegal entry of a person or persons across an international border, in violation of one or more countries' laws, either clandestinely or through deception, such as the use of fraudulent documents.

involuntary domestic servitude—A form of forced labor involving domestic workers in private residences. Such an environment, which often socially isolates domestic workers, is conducive to exploitation because authorities cannot inspect private property as easily as formal workplaces.

involuntary servitude—Under the TVPA, includes a condition of servitude induced by means of (1) any scheme, plan, or pattern intended to cause a person to believe that, if the person did not enter into or continue in such condition, that person or another person would suffer serious harm or physical restraint or (2) the abuse or threatened abuse of the legal process.

labor trafficking—Under the TVPA, the recruitment, harboring, transportation, provision, or obtaining of a person for labor or services through the use of force, fraud, or coercion for the purposes of subjection to involuntary servitude, peonage, debt bondage, or slavery.

Mann Act (1910)—Makes it a felony to knowingly transport any person in interstate or foreign commerce for prostitution, or for any sexual activity for which a person can be charged with a criminal offense. A person also violates the act if he persuades, induces, entices, or coerces an individual to travel across state lines to engage in prostitution or other immoral purposes, or attempts to do so.

minor—Under the TVPA, any person under the age of eighteen.

National Human Trafficking Resource Center (NHTRC)—A national, toll-free hotline, available to answer calls from anywhere in the United States twenty-four hours a day, seven days a week, every day of the year. It is operated by Polaris Project, a nongovernmental organization working to combat human trafficking. Callers can report tips and receive information on human trafficking by calling the hotline at 888-373-7888. The hotline also provides data on where cases of suspected human trafficking are occurring in the United States.

National Slavery and Human Protection Month—Established by a presidential proclamation declaring January as National Slavery and Human Trafficking Prevention Month. January 12 already marks National Global Human Trafficking Awareness Day in the United States.

Organization of American States (OAS)—Maintains an anti-trafficking section that works to aggregate national efforts, bilateral measures, and multilateral cooperation. The section provides information for training seminars, technical assistance to governments, exchange of information, and proposals.

pimp—A person who controls and financially benefits from the commercial sexual exploitation of another person. The relationship can be abusive and possessive, with the pimp using techniques such as psychological intimidation, manipulation, starvation, rape, gang rape, beating, confinement, threats of violence toward the victim's family, forced drug use, and the shame from these acts to keep the sexually exploited person under control.

President's Interagency Task Force to Monitor and Combat Human Trafficking (PITF)—A cabinet-level entity created by the TVPA to coordinate federal efforts to combat trafficking in persons. The PITF meets annually and is chaired by the secretary of state.

PROTECT Act (2003)—Enacted to combat the sexual exploitation of children, the act requires courts to impose mandatory sentences for sex offenders and makes it a crime to travel abroad to engage in sexual conduct with minors. The act amends the criminal code to increase supervision of convicted sex offenders for specific felonies and creates minimum standards and grants for states to expand their Amber Alert system for missing children.

The Protocol to Prevent, Suppress and Punish Trafficking in Persons, Especially Women and Children—Also referred to as the "Trafficking Protocol," it was adopted by the UN in 2000 and is an international legal agreement attached to the UN Convention Against Transnational Organized Crime. The protocol sets out an agreed definition of trafficking in persons. The purpose of the protocol is to facilitate convergence in national cooperation in investigating and prosecuting trafficking in persons and protect and assist the victims.

self-generated child sexual abuse material (SG-CSAM)—Sexual imagery of a child that appears to have been taken by the child in the image. This imagery can result from both consensual and coercive experiences.

sex industry—Consists of businesses that either directly or indirectly provide sex-related products and services or adult entertainment.

sex tourism—The World Tourism Organization, a specialized agency of the UN, defines sex tourism as "trips organized from within the tourism sector, or from outside this sector but using its structures and networks, with the primary purpose of effecting a commercial sexual relationship by the tourist with residents at the destination."

sex trafficking—Under the TVPA, the recruitment, harboring, transportation, provision, or obtaining of a person for the purposes of a commercial sex act, in which the commercial sex act is induced by force, fraud, or coercion, or in which the person induced to perform such an act has not attained eighteen years of age.

T visa—Created under the TVPA, the T visa gives temporary nonimmigrant status to victims of severe forms of trafficking on the condition that they help law enforcement officials investigate and prosecute crimes related to human trafficking. If the victim, however, is under eighteen years of age, the law does not require cooperation with police. The applicant must show that he or she (1) is a victim of trafficking, (2) is in the United States without status due to trafficking, (3) complies with any reasonable request from a law enforcement agency for assistance in the investigation or prosecution of human trafficking, and (4) would suffer extreme hardship involving unusual and severe harm if removed from the United States. T visas are also available for immediate family members, including spouses, children, and parents of applicants under eighteen. Only five thousand T visas may be issued every year.

***Trafficking in Persons Report* (*TIP Report*)**—Tracks the anti-trafficking efforts of every foreign country. The US government uses the *TIP Report* to engage foreign governments in dialogues to advance anti-trafficking reforms and target resources on prevention, protection, and prosecution programs. In the *TIP Report*, the Department of

State places each country onto one of three tiers based on the extent of their governments' efforts to comply with the "minimum standards for the elimination of trafficking."

Trafficking Victims Protection Act (TVPA) (2000)—The first comprehensive federal law to address human trafficking, the act provided a three-pronged approach to combating human trafficking: prevention through public awareness programs and a monitoring and sanctions program led by the Department of State, protection through visas and services for foreign-national victims, and prosecution through new federal crimes. This legislation was reauthorized in 2003, 2005, and 2008.

U visa—A nonimmigrant visa granting work eligibility to certain victims of crimes occurring in the United States. The applicant must have suffered substantial physical or mental abuse due to certain criminal activities including trafficking, prostitution, sexual exploitation, rape, involuntary servitude, slave trade, or kidnapping. Victims must also be willing to work with local law enforcement and obtain certification by a federal, state, or local law enforcement agency, such as a prosecutor or a federal or state judge in charge of the investigation in which the petitioner is the victim. Only ten thousand U visas may be issued every fiscal year. Family members, including spouses, children, unmarried sisters and brothers under eighteen, mothers, fathers, stepparents, and adoptive parents, may also be included on the petition.

United Nations Office on Drugs and Crime (UNODC)—UN office that enforces the Convention Against Transnational Organized Crime (a.k.a. the Palermo Convention).

US Citizenship and Immigration Services (USCIS)—Processes both T and U visa applications.

US Immigration and Customs Enforcement (ICE)—Agency powered to investigate and apprehend traffickers. They also provide or assist victims with obtaining services.

Appendix B

FEMA LETTER TO FAITH LEADERS

FROM FEMA (FEDERAL EMERGENCY MANAGEMENT AGENCY) IN RESPONSE TO THE 20TH ANNIVERSARY OF THE PASSAGE OF THE TRAFFICKING VICTIMS PROTECTION ACT OF 2000

THIS LETTER PROVIDES AN EXAMPLE of how the government partners with faith communities and churches in the work to end human trafficking.

October 28, 2020

Dear Faith and Community Leaders,

Twenty years ago today, on October 28, with the enactment of federal law, our nation began what was to be a united effort to examine the depth and magnitude of human trafficking, or trafficking in persons, throughout communities in the United States. Prior to this time, we did not have the name "human trafficking" or a universal definition for the harsh treatment of people who are sexually exploited, forced to work in inhumane conditions or for individuals and communities that are adversely impacted by this kind of maltreatment and violence.

Due in part to the tireless efforts and overwhelming support of faith and community leaders and countless other public and private sectors serving victims of this crime, today, along with you, we remember the 20th Anniversary of the passage of the Trafficking Victims Protection Act (TVPA) of 2000. The TVPA is the first federal law in the United States to address the transnational crime of human trafficking, child sexual exploitation and forced labor.

We stood up and fought against the harms of those exploited for profit or gain—and even now, we continue to work hard to protect their human dignity, rights and freedom.

Also, in 2000, the United Nations adopted the Palermo Protocol to Prevent, Suppress and Punish Trafficking in Persons, Especially Women and Children, a universal instrument that addresses all aspects of trafficking in persons who are vulnerable to trafficking.

As a result of the TVPA, over the past 20 years, the federal government has played a major role in countering human trafficking. The federal government's response across departments and agencies have joined together in a whole-of-government approach that addresses all aspects of human trafficking by creating the cabinet-level President's Interagency Task Force to Monitor and Combat Trafficking in Persons, the Senior Policy Operating Group and numerous resources.

Today, the federal government continues to develop new policies and criminal and labor laws. Through research and better tracking techniques, we've made substantial progress in victim identification and protection measures. Educational programs, such as DHS Blue Campaign and HHS Look Beneath the Surface, significantly enhanced the public's awareness of human trafficking.

Furthermore, the White House recently released the National Action Plan to Combat Human Trafficking to direct the federal government's efforts to end human trafficking within the United States. In addition, the Department of Justice's Office of Justice Programs demonstrated its commitment to anti–human trafficking by awarding more than $100 million in grant funding to task forces combatting human trafficking as well as victim services and safe and stable housing organizations. And, on Oct. 15, 2020, the Department of Homeland Security Center for Faith and Opportunity Initiatives hosted a webinar highlighting the contributions of our frontline faith and community leaders who diligently work to counter human trafficking in all of its forms.

Ten years ago, the US Department of Homeland Security (DHS) committed to working collectively across departmental agencies on a national public awareness campaign, known as the DHS Blue Campaign. The campaign educates the public, law enforcement and other industry partners to recognize the indicators of human trafficking and how to appropriately respond to possible cases.

The Blue Campaign develops training and materials to help increase detection of human trafficking and to identify victims. In particular, the Faith-Based and Community Toolkit, a human trafficking toolkit for the faith community developed in partnership with the DHS Center, is available in both English and Spanish with a complementary General Awareness Training Video. Many of you throughout the years have helped us to share public awareness messages and training to educate the public on the atrocities of human trafficking, sexual exploitation and forced labor, providing resources on how to get help and report this crime to law enforcement.

With these achievements, we have cause to celebrate. And, there is yet another milestone. We are excited to share the opening of the new Center for Countering Human Trafficking (CCHT) in the Department of Homeland Security. The vision to develop a new center was cited in the DHS Strategy to Combat Human Trafficking, the Importation of Goods Produced with Forced Labor, and Child Sexual Exploitation. The Center is the U.S. Government's first integrated law enforcement operations center directly supporting federal criminal investigations, victim assistance, intelligence analysis, and outreach and training related to human trafficking and the importation of goods produced by forced labor.

The Center is established as a multi-component organization, consolidating and synchronizing 16 DHS programs. This Center stands committed to disrupting and dismantling human trafficking organizations and providing support and protection to victims. Similar to the TVPA, the Center's approach to combatting human trafficking is rooted in prevention, protection, prosecution and strategic partnerships. To contact the Center for Countering Human Trafficking please submit inquiries to CCHT@hq.dhs.gov.

For all the faith and community leaders who have served on the frontlines over the past 20 years (and more) as well as medical professionals and social service providers, we thank you for your unwavering commitment. To those who advocate and stand alongside people in need of food, shelter, employment, education, and a daily dose of encouragement, you have been the bedrock of the program's success. To those in law enforcement or who provide legal representation to counter the atrocities of trafficking, you have been a pillar of strength. We are deeply grateful to you all. Thank you for raising your voices and continuing to speak about this unspeakable injustice. We value your commitment to human dignity, humanity and freedom. Together, we will keep working to bring an end to human trafficking, sexual exploitation and forced labor in our lifetime.

In service,
Nicole C. Wood, MPH, MA
U.S. Department of Homeland Security
DHS Center for Faith and Opportunity Initiatives

Appendix C

FAITH AND FREEDOM POLICY BRIEF

THE IMPORTANT ROLE OF LOCAL FAITH ACTORS IN ANTI-HUMAN TRAFFICKING AND ANTI-MODERN SLAVERY

THIS APPENDIX PROVIDES AN EXAMPLE of research being conducted regarding the importance of local faith actors (LFAs)—including churches—in the fight to end human trafficking. The Faith and Freedom Policy Brief was developed by the Joint Learning Initiatives on Faith & Local Communities (JLI) from a scoping study titled *Faith and Freedom: The Role of Faith Actors in Anti-Modern Slavery and Human Trafficking*.[1] Excerpts of the policy brief presented here provide specific examples of collaboration and recommendations taken from that study.

THE ROLE OF LOCAL FAITH ACTORS

In coordination with global efforts, we assert that local faith actors (LFAs)—which can include formal and informal religious leaders, worship communities, faith networks, and local and national faith-based organizations from a variety of religions—play an imperative role in the implementation and sustainability of human trafficking interventions at every level.

POSSIBLE PURPOSES OF THIS BRIEF

1. To share evidence with LFAs that affirms their critical role in anti-trafficking work and that they may acquire different levels of support from policymakers and funders.

2. To inform LFAs who are not actively engaging in Anti–Human Trafficking and Modern Slavery (AHT-MS) or are less familiar with human trafficking about their important role as local faith-based organizations.
3. To convince multilateral organizations of the imperative role of LFAs in AHT work in order to spur greater investment in and collaboration with LFAs in the global AHT response.

OVERVIEW

Given the vital role that faith communities play in ending human trafficking and modern slavery, the JLI Anti–Human Trafficking and Modern Slavery (AHT-MS) Hub Scoping Study—Faith and Freedom—published in 2019, examined the involvement of LFAs in addressing human trafficking in the Global South. The study methodology included an in-depth review of over 200 pieces of gray and academic literature and fourteen practitioner interviews. Recognizing the Palermo Protocol's 3P paradigm (prosecution, protection and prevention), fundamental to holistically addressing AHT-MS, the study found evidence of constructive LFA involvement in every method of human trafficking intervention, often contributing in ways that would be extremely difficult or impossible for international or secular actors to accomplish. . . .

The study supports the view that people of faith, with their unique community presence, connection, and ability to respond to needs, are critical to effectively and sustainably responding to human trafficking around the world. We assert that an effective AHT-MS plan is incomplete without a comprehensive plan to include LFAs in the intervention strategy through the means of, though not limited to, training for, funding to, and the judicial participation of LFAs.

LESSONS LEARNED

- **"More widely classifying [development] programming as Prevention may increase the likelihood of funding being appropriated to it."**
  - This is because LFAs do not always know how to articulate what they are doing in terms of language understood by donors. . . .

- **"Religious leaders [are] people of positive influence who will help their communities take human trafficking and modern slavery seriously."**
  - Acknowledging the societal influence of LFAs, Islamic Relief is planning a project in Nepal to "engage Hindu and Islamic leaders in several ways, such as in forums, in the media, and through door-to-door awareness campaigns." . . .
- **LFAs can be uniquely positioned to aid in the prosecutorial process in ways other actors cannot.**
  - "Police in India . . . involve Catholic sisters [from Talitha Kum] when they conduct anti-trafficking raids, given that their testimony is taken as credible and trusted in court." . . .
- **LFAs are "critical to sustaining systemic [policy] changes" as they involve large, influential networks that never leave the country.**
  - The Philippine Interfaith Movement Against Human Trafficking is a partnership created between the three largest ecclesiastical councils in the Philippines and their networks, all committed to working together against human trafficking. . . .
- **Partnering with LFAs allows for rapid community mobilization of existing faith networks and strong grassroots participation.**
  - HAART Kenya (a secular NGO) chooses to "work with both Christians and Muslims as main partners" to gain access to trusted networks and grassroots support. . . .

CASE STUDIES

1. Brick Kiln Owners in Northern India

Many families in Northern India live in generational debt bondage under brick kiln owners, owing thousands of dollars with little hope of ever paying off their debts. Living in poor conditions and without access to public education, children work alongside their parents for ten to twelve hours daily in extreme heat with insufficient nourishment. Acknowledging these needs, Catholic sisters have provided non-formal education programs for the children, general health and medical services, and basic adult life skills courses for brick kiln workers.

While brick kiln owners are generally hostile to outsiders providing services for their workers—fearing they will gain the capacity to speak up for themselves or run away—the persistence of the sisters to serve, as well as their status as religious figures, has allowed them access to these otherwise heavily protected facilities. Access to those in debt bondage in India, which would be a highly difficult feat for NGOs, has been granted to the sisters on the basis of their locality to the region as well as their religiosity. . . .

Lessons Learned:

- Although there can be small returns on initiatives that serve trafficking survivors, the value of these services is in the relational aspects of the services, which faith-based care is perceived to do well.
- Local faith actors can provide an important level of persistence in anti-human trafficking work due to their religious convictions and long-term commitment to the communities in which they live.

2. Interfaith Collaboration

In 2013, the International Justice Mission organized "The Freedom Forum" in Manila, Philippines, a conference that included seven hundred leaders from large Protestant, evangelical, and Catholic networks in the country. The forum launched a national initiative called "The Philippine Interfaith Movement Against Human Trafficking (PIMAHT)," which created a formal partnership between the three largest ecclesiastical councils in the Philippines and their networks, all committed to working together against human trafficking.

PIMAHT has worked closely with NGOs and governmental entities and has been instrumental in mobilizing Philippine churches to own human trafficking as an issue they care about, to reduce duplication of and streamline AHT-MS services, and to expand programmatic impact. PIMAHT additionally organizes large conferences that bring together many actors around the table, both faith-based and secular, to discuss human trafficking and collaborate on ways to move forward. . . .

Apart from PIMAHT, our scoping study has identified other instances of important interfaith collaborations such as:

- HAART Kenya (a secular NGO) works with Christians and Muslims as main partners to allow for more rapid mobilization and community trust. For example, HAART holds workshops on child trafficking and other human rights issues in the churches and mosques of faith groups with which they partner. . . .
- World Vision partners with Buddhist leaders in Cambodia through their Channels of Hope project. This builds the capacity of the faith community, largely including monks, to address harmful practices including human trafficking. . . .

Lessons Learned

- A need continues to exist for religious leaders to be educated on these matters so they may distribute this knowledge to their large networks and trusted communities.
- LFAs have access to existing community structures for creating awareness, making them effective at distributing AHT messaging.
- INGO and governmental partnerships with LFAs provide the needed resources (financial and technical) to LFAs, while leaving the programmatic execution to those already established in the community.

3. LFA Prosecution Efforts

A 2018 symposium in Indonesia brought together legal experts and professionals from Indonesia Rights for Women along with Catholic sisters, a Franciscan Seminarian, a Muslim woman, and a Protestant clergyman in order to build their legal capacities in service. The Catholic sisters, in particular, could not attend criminal proceedings to speak up for victims of human trafficking because they lacked the professional qualifications to do so. The seminar supported participants in learning what they need to do to be able to engage in the judicial process, and to create a standard operating procedure. . . .

Apart from the Indonesian symposium, we have found additional meaningful engagement of LFAs in the judicial space, including:

- Catholic sisters are participating in anti-trafficking raids in India because it is easier to obtain prosecution with the trusted testimony of sisters. . . .

- The Santa Marta group prioritizes forming partnerships with local faith actors because they have found that victims turn to trusted religious figures in the community to share information that they would not share with law enforcement. Such relationally based sharing with religious figures helps law enforcement gain credible information about ongoing criminal activity. . . .

Lessons Learned

- The testimony of LFAs could have a unique and trusted voice in court, making them valuable participants in judicial proceedings.
- Victims may be willing to share key information with LFAs that they would not share with others, which could be instrumental in forming a criminal case.
- Many LFAs desire to be involved and could meaningfully assist in prosecutorial processes, but lack the necessary skills to do so.

Our research findings from the scoping study strongly support that LFAs are strong assets in the global collaborative effort to counter human trafficking, leading us to the following policy recommendations:

- Funders should invest in the frontline work of LFAs, even if they do not have the typical organizational structure valued by mainstream donors, as this work provides an integral preventative element in AHT-MS work.
- Policy stakeholders and funders should promote partnerships between prosecutorial agencies (e.g. police and judiciary) and local faith actors that can add value to their work in prosecuting traffickers and supporting survivors through the judicial process.
- Funders should invest in technical training (in judicial proceedings, trauma-informed care, etc.) to improve the skills of LFAs dedicated to supporting survivors and people vulnerable to HT-MS.
- LFAs should be more widely understood as sustainable partners for either new anti-trafficking programming, or as partners for existing initiatives, as engaging the local faith community is key to sustaining systemic changes and widening influence and impact.

- Those concerned about modern slavery and human trafficking should engage high-level religious leaders and LFAs, and high-level religious leaders should engage with LFAs at the grassroots level, to ensure mutual commitment to actively contribute to, and engage with, anti-modern-slavery and anti-human-trafficking.
- The Scoping Study found constructive LFA involvement in categories other than the Palermo's 3P Paradigm. We instead propose considering a Freedom Framework which recognizes additional areas of response, including prevention, protection, prosecution, policy, partnership, participation, prayer and proof.

NOTES

INTRODUCTION: BUILD A SAFETY FENCE

[1]US Department of State, "International and Domestic Law," Office to Monitor and Combat Trafficking in Persons, US Department of State, accessed July 29, 2021, www.state.gov/international-and-domestic-law. "Protocol to Prevent, Suppress and Punish Trafficking in Persons Especially Women and Children, Supplementing the United Nations Convention against Transnational Organized Crime," United Nations Human Rights, Office of the High Commissioner, November 15, 2000, www.ohchr.org/en/professionalinterest/pages/protocoltraffickinginpersons.aspx.

[2]John McKnight and John Kretzman, *Building Communities from the Inside Out* (Chicago: ACTA Publications, 1993).

1. ELEMENTS AND TYPES OF HUMAN TRAFFICKING

[1]United Nations Office on Drugs and Crime, *United Nations Convention Against Transnational Organized Crime and the Protocols Thereto* (New York: United Nations, 2004), www.unodc.org/documents/treaties/UNTOC/Publications/TOC%20Convention/TOCebook-e.pdf.

[2]United Nations Office on Drugs and Crime, *United Nations Convention Against Transnational Organized Crime.*

[3]International Labour Organization and Walk Free Foundation, *Global Estimates of Modern Slavery: Forced Labour and Forced Marriage* (Geneva: International Labour Office, 2017), www.ilo.org/wcmsp5/groups/public/@dgreports/@dcomm/documents/publication/wcms_575479.pdf.

[4]International Labour Organization and Walk Free Foundation, *Global Estimates of Modern Slavery.*

[5]"Fact Sheet: Labor Trafficking," Office on Trafficking in Persons, US Department of Health & Human Services Administration for Children and Families, accessed May 24, 2021, www.acf.hhs.gov/archive/otip/resource/fact-sheet-labor-trafficking-english.

[6]"Fact Sheet: Labor Trafficking," Office on Trafficking in Persons.

[7]International Labour Organization and Walk Free Foundation, *Global Estimates of Modern Slavery.*

[8]"Domestic Work," National Human Trafficking Hotline, accessed May 24, 2021, humantraffickinghotline.org/labor-trafficking-venuesindustries/domestic-work.

[9]*Hidden Slaves: Forced Labor in the United States,* Free the Slaves and Human Rights Center, September 2004, www.freetheslaves.net/wp-content/uploads/2015/03/Hidden-Slaves.pdf.

[10]Kevin Bales and Ron Soodalter, *The Slave Next Door* (Berkeley: University of California Press, 2009), 255.

[11]Sandie Morgan, Dave Stachowiak, and Rachel Thomas, "196—Rachel Thomas: Ending the Game," April 14, 2019, *Ending Human Trafficking* podcast, endinghumantrafficking.org/podcast/196.

[12]Julia Wolfe, Jori Kandra, Lora Engdaul, and Heidi Shierholz, "Domestic Workers Chartbook" Economic Policy Institute, May 14, 2020, www.epi.org/publication/domestic-workers-chartbook-a-comprehensive-look-at-the-demographics-wages-benefits-and-poverty-rates-of-the-professionals-who-care-for-our-family-members-and-clean-our-homes.

[13]"Domestic Work," National Human Trafficking Hotline.

[14]"Domestic Work," National Human Trafficking Hotline.

[15]Wolfe, Kandra, Engdaul, and Shierholz, "Domestic Workers Chartbook."

[16]"Domestic Work," National Human Trafficking Hotline.

[17]Bales and Soodalter, *Slave Next Door,* 47.

[18]"Farm Labor," Economic Research Service, US Department of Agriculture, April 22, 2020, www.ers.usda.gov/topics/farm-economy/farm-labor/#size.

[19]"Human Trafficking on Temporary Work Visas: A Data Analysis 2015–2017," Polaris, April 2018, polarisproject.org/wp-content/uploads/2019/01/Human-Trafficking-on-Temporary-Work-Visas.pdf.

[20]Sean Sellers and Greg Asbed, "The History and Evolution of Forced Labor in Florida Agriculture," *Race/Ethnicity: Multidisciplinary Global Contexts* 5, no. 1 (2011): 29-49. Gaia Pianigiani, "A Woman's Death Sorting Grapes Exposes Italy's 'Slavery,'" *New York Times,* April 11, 2017, www.nytimes.com/2017/04/11/world/europe/a-womans-death-sorting-grapes-exposes-italys-slavery.html. "Human Trafficking and Farmworkers," Freedom Network USA, March 2013, freedomnetworkusa.org/app/uploads/2016/12/Farmworkers.pdf. Sabrina Pecorelli, "The Hidden Ingredient in Chocolate: Africa's Child Slaves," *Charged Affairs,* April 27, 2020, chargedaffairs.org/the-hidden-ingredient-in-chocolate-africas-child-slaves. "Uzbekistan: Forced Labor Linked to World Bank," Human Rights Watch, June 27, 2017, www.hrw.org/news/2017/06/27/uzbekistan-forced-labor-linked-world-bank.

[21]"Cotton," Responsible Sourcing Network, accessed May 24, 2021, www.sourcingnetwork.org/cotton.

[22]"2018 List of Goods Produced by Child Labor and Forced Labor," US Department of Labor, 2018, www.dol.gov/sites/dolgov/files/ILAB/ListofGoods.pdf.

[23]Siddharth Kara, "Is Your Phone Tainted by the Misery of the Children in Congo's Mines?" *The Guardian*, October 12, 2018, www.theguardian.com/global-development/2018/oct/12/phone-misery-children-congo-cobalt-mines-drc. Annie Callaway, "Powering Down Corruption: Tackling Transparency and Human Rights Risks from Congo's Cobalt Mines to Global Supply Chains," Enough Project, October 2018, enoughproject.org/wp-content/uploads/PoweringDownCorruption_Enough_Oct2018-web.pdf. "Progress and Challenges on Conflict Minerals," Enough Project, accessed May 24, 2021, enoughproject.org/special-topics/progress-and-challenges-conflict-minerals-facts-dodd-frank-1502.

[24]"Children Recruited by Armed Forces," UNICEF, accessed May 24, 2021, www.unicef.org/protection/children-recruited-by-armed-forces.

[25]*Trafficking in Persons Report: June 2019*, US Department of State, 2019, www.state.gov/wp-content/uploads/2019/06/2019-Trafficking-in-Persons-Report.pdf.

[26]*Hidden Chains: Rights Abuses and Forced Labor in Thailand's Fishing Industry*, Human Rights Watch, January 23, 2018, www.hrw.org/report/2018/01/23/hidden-chains/rights-abuses-and-forced-labor-thailands-fishing-industry.

[27]Ian Urbina, "Sea Slaves: The Human Misery that Feeds Pets and Livestock," *New York Times*, July 27, 2015, www.nytimes.com/2015/07/27/world/outlaw-ocean-thailand-fishing-sea-slaves-pets.html.

[28]"Agreement of Port State Measures (PSMA)," Food and Agriculture Organization of the United Nations, June 2016, www.fao.org/port-state-measures/en.

[29]"Seafood Slavery Risk Tool," March 2020, libertyshared.org/ssrt-beta.

[30]"Global Slavery Index 2018," Walk Free Foundation, 2018, www.globalslaveryindex.org.

[31]"2018 List of Goods Produced by Child Labor and Forced Labor," US Department of Labor.

[32]"Restaurants/Food Service," National Human Trafficking Hotline, accessed July 29, 2021, humantraffickinghotline.org/es/labor-trafficking-venuesindustries/restaurants food-service.

[33]"Harkin Engel Protocol," International Cocoa Initiative, October 4, 2001, cocoainitiative.org/knowledge-centre-post/harkin-engel-protocol. "Protocol for the Growing and Processing of Cocoa Beans and Their Derivative Products in a Manner that Complies with the ILO Convention 182 Concerning the Prohibition and Immediate Action for the Elimination of the Worst Forms of Child Labor," International Cocoa Initiative, September 19, 2001, cocoainitiative.org/wp-content/uploads/2016/10/Harkin_Engel_Protocol.pdf.

[34]"Framework of Action to Support Implementation of the Harkin-Engel Protocol," International Cocoa Initiative, accessed May 25, 2021, cocoainitiative.org/wp-content/uploads/2016/10/Cocoa_Framework_of_Action_9-12-10_Final-1-1.pdf.

[35]Abbie Uychiat, "Bad Chocolate: Hershey's, Nestle, and Mars Inc. Are Facing Child Slavery Accusations," *Food World News*, October 6, 2015, www.foodworldnews.com/articles/42109/20151006/shocking-child-slavery-claims-regarding-major-chocolate-companies-the-hershey-company-nestle-and-mars-inc.htm.

[36]*Putting Children First: International Cocoa Initiative 2019 Annual Report*, International Cocoa Initiative, 2019, annualreport2019.cocoainitiative.org/en.

[37]Peter Whoriskey and Rachel Siegel, "Cocoa's Child Laborers," *Washington Post*, June 5, 2019, www.washingtonpost.com/graphics/2019/business/hershey-nestle-mars-chocolate-child-labor-west-africa.

[38]Whoriskey and Siegel, "Cocoa's Child Laborers."

[39]"Child Labour in Cocoa," International Cocoa Initiative, 2021, www.cocoainitiative.org/issues/child-labour-cocoa.

[40]"Trafficking in Persons for the Purpose of Organ Removal," United Nations Office on Drugs and Crime, 2015, www.unodc.org/documents/human-trafficking/2015/UNODC_Assessment_Toolkit_TIP_for_the_Purpose_of_Organ_Removal.pdf.

[41]Siddarth Kara, *Sex Trafficking: Inside the Business of Modern Slavery* (New York: Columbia University Press, 2009), 19.

[42]Hannabeth Fanchino-Olsen, "Vulnerabilities Relevant for Commercial Sexual Exploitation of Children/Domestic Minor Sex Trafficking: A Systematic Review of Risk Factors," *Trauma, Violence, & Abuse* 22, no. 1 (January 2021): 99-111.

[43]Rachel Swaner et al., "Youth Involvement in the Sex Trade: A National Study," Center For Court Innovation, June 2016, www.ncjrs.gov/pdffiles1/ojjdp/grants/249952.pdf.

[44]Rachel Lloyd, *Girls Like Us: Fighting for a World Where Girls Are Not for Sale* (New York: HarperCollins, 2011), 78.

[45]Adapted from Rebecca Bender and Sandie Morgan, "234—Relentless Advocate: Rebecca Bender," October 5, 2020, *Ending Human Trafficking* podcast, endinghumantrafficking.org/podcast/234-relentless-advocate-rebecca-bender.

[46]"About Child Marriage," Girls Not Brides, 2021, www.girlsnotbrides.org/about-child-marriage.

[47]"Child Marriage," April 2020, UNICEF, data.unicef.org/topic/child-protection/child-marriage.

[48]Adapted from Sandie Morgan, Dave Stachowiak, and Diana Mao, "227—Another Form of Human Trafficking: Child and Forced Marriage," *Ending Human Trafficking* podcast, endinghumantrafficking.org/podcast/227.

[49]Melissa Farely, "Prostitution, Trafficking, and Cultural Amnesia: What We Must Not Know in Order to Keep the Business of Sexual Exploitation Running Smoothly," *Yale Journal of Law and Feminism* 18, no. 109 (2006): 109-44.

[50]"Prostitution Facts," RapeIs.org, accessed May 26, 2021, www.rapeis.org/activism/prostitution/prostitutionfacts.html.

[51]Victor Malarek, *The Johns: Sex for Sale and the Men Who Buy It* (New York: Arcade, 2009), 197.

[52]"The Scourge of Child Pornography: Working to Stop the Sexual Exploitation of Children," FBI, April 25, 2017, www.fbi.gov/news/stories/the-scourge-of-child-pornography.

[53]Julie Cordua, "A Letter from Our CEO: Julie Cordua on Thorn's response to COVID-19,"

Thorn, April 30, 2020, www.thorn.org/blog/a-letter-from-our-ceo-julie-cordua-on-thorns-response-to-covid-19.

[54]"What's the Average Age of a Child's First Exposure to Porn," Fight the New Drug, November 23, 2020, fightthenewdrug.org/real-average-age-of-first-exposure.

2. PAST AND PRESENT

[1]Mark Cartwright, "Slavery in the Roman World," *World History Encyclopedia*, November 1, 2013, www.ancient.eu/article/629/slavery-in-the-roman-world.

[2]Kevin Bales, *Disposable People* (Berkeley: University of California Press, 1999), 8.

[3]*Trafficking in Persons Report: June 2019*, US Department of State, June 2019, www.state.gov/wp-content/uploads/2019/06/2019-Trafficking-in-Persons-Report.pdf.

[4]James Montgomery Boice, *Hosea–Jonah*, vol. 1 of *The Minor Prophets* (Grand Rapids, MI: Baker Books, 1983), 163.

[5]*Trafficking in Persons Report: 20th Edition*, US Department of State, June 2020, www.state.gov/wp-content/uploads/2020/06/2020-TIP-Report-Complete-062420-FINAL.pdf.

[6]"Protocol to Prevent, Suppress and Punish Trafficking in Persons, Especially Women and Children, Supplementing the United Nations Convention Against Transnational Organized Crime," United Nations, December 2000, www.ohchr.org/Documents/ProfessionalInterest/ProtocolonTrafficking.pdf.

[7]*Trafficking in Persons Report: 20th Edition*, US Department of State.

[8]"Global Slavery Index 2018," Walk Free Foundation, 2018, www.globalslaveryindex.org.

[9]"Forced Labour, Modern Slavery and Human Trafficking," International Labour Organization, 2021, www.ilo.org/global/topics/forced-labour/lang--en/index.htm.

3. PREVENTION

[1]Details of this account are taken from Sandra Morgan and Dave Stachowiak, "148—We Are Back to the Language: Labels Matter," *Ending Human Trafficking* podcast, July 2, 2017, endinghumantrafficking.org/podcast/148.

[2]Morgan and Stachowiak, "We Are Back to the Language."

[3]"What Fuels Human Trafficking?" UNICEF USA, January 13, 2017, www.unicefusa.org/stories/what-fuels-human-trafficking/31692.

[4]Siddharth Kara, *Modern Slavery: A Global Perspective* (New York: Columbia University Press, 2017), 148.

[5]Monique Villa, "Women Own Less Than 20% of the World's Land. It's Time to Give Them Equal Property Rights," World Economic Forum, January 11, 2017, www.weforum.org/agenda/2017/01/women-own-less-than-20-of-the-worlds-land-its-time-to-give-them-equal-property-rights.

[6]Villa, "Women Own Less Than 20%."

[7]"Invisible Women, Invisible Problems," International Widows' Day June 23, United Nations, accessed May 30, 2021, www.un.org/en/observances/widows-day.

[8]"Natural Disasters and the Increased Risk for Human Trafficking," *Polaris* (blog),

September 1, 2017, polarisproject.org/blog/2017/09/natural-disasters-and-the-increased-risk-for-human-trafficking.

[9]*Public Private Partnership Advisory Council to End Human Trafficking 2020 Annual Report*, US Department of State, 2020, www.state.gov/wp-content/uploads/2020/11/public-private-partnership-advisory-council-to-end-human-trafficking-2020-annual-report.pdf.

[10]"Commercial Sexual Exploitation of Children," Office of Juvenile Justice and Delinquency Prevention, accessed June 1, 2021, ojjdp.ojp.gov/programs/commercial-sexual-exploitation-children.

[11]"The Developmental Assets Framework," Search Institute, *copyright* 2021, www.search-institute.org/our-research/development-assets/developmental-assets-framework.

[12]Sandra Morgan and Dave Stachowiak, "109—Prevention: Saving Up for a Rainy Day," *Ending Human Trafficking* podcast, October 1, 2015, endinghumantrafficking.org/podcast/109.

[13]Adapted from Sandie Morgan, Dave Stachowiak, and Tracy Webb, "69—Cyber Crimes and Brittany's Story," *Ending Human Trafficking* podcast, November 28, 2013, endinghumantrafficking.org/podcast/69.

[14]"Understanding the Teen Brain," University of Rochester Medical Center, 2021, www.urmc.rochester.edu/encyclopedia/content.aspx?ContentTypeID=1&ContentID=3051.

[15]Steven L. West and Keri K. O'Neal, "Project D.A.R.E. Outcome Effectiveness Revisited," *American Journal of Public Health* 94, no. 6 (June 2004): 1027-29.

[16]*2019 Data Report: The U.S. National Human Trafficking Hotline*, Polaris, December 31, 2019, humantraffickinghotline.org/sites/default/files/Polaris-2019-US-National-Human-Trafficking-Hotline-Data-Report.pdf.

[17]Adapted from Sandie Morgan, Dave Stachowiak, and Derek Marsh, "71—A Dozen Myths About Human Trafficking (Part 1)," *Ending Human Trafficking* podcast, December 26, 2013, endinghumantrafficking.org/podcast/71.

[18]John McKnight, "Asset-Based Community Development: The Essentials," ABCD Institute, 2017, resources.depaul.edu/abcd-institute/publications/publications-by-topic/Documents/ABCD-%20The%20Essentials%20-2.pdf.

[19]McKnight, "Asset-Based Community Development."

[20]LaCinda Bloomfield, *Frontline Woman* (LaCinda Bloomfield Communications, 2019), 135-36.

4. PROTECTION

[1]Shayne Moore and Kimberly McOwen Yim, *Refuse to Do Nothing* (Downers Grove, IL: InterVarsity Press, 2013), 103.

[2]Heather J. Clawson, Amy Salomon, and Lisa Goldblatt Grace, "Treating the Hidden Wounds: Trauma Treatment and Mental Health Recovery for Victims of Human Trafficking," Office of the Assistant Secretary for Planning and Evaluation, US Department of Health and Human Services, March 15, 2008, aspe.hhs.gov/reports/treating-hidden-wounds-trauma-treatment-and-mental-health-recovery-victims-human-trafficking-0.

[3]"About the CDC-Kaiser ACE Study," Centers for Disease Control and Prevention, updated April 6, 2021, www.cdc.gov/violenceprevention/aces/about.html.

[4]"SAMHSA's Concept of Trauma and Guidance for a Trauma-Informed Approach," Substance Abuse and Mental Health Services Administration, US Department of Health and Human Services, July 2014, ncsacw.samhsa.gov/userfiles/files/SAMHSA_Trauma.pdf. Tim Hein, *Understanding Sexual Abuse* (Downers Grove, IL: InterVarsity Press, 2018).

[5]"Trauma and Violence," Substance Abuse and Mental Health Services Administration, US Department of Health and Human Services, updated August 2, 2019, www.samhsa.gov/trauma-violence.

[6]"SAMHSA's Concept of Trauma and Guidance for a Trauma-Informed Approach," Substance Abuse and Mental Health Services Administration.

[7]"SAMHSA's Concept of Trauma and Guidance for a Trauma-Informed Approach," Substance Abuse and Mental Health Services Administration.

[8]"SAMHSA's Concept of Trauma and Guidance for a Trauma-Informed Approach," Substance Abuse and Mental Health Services Administration.

[9]"Creating Trauma-Informed Care Environments: Organizational Self-Assessment for Trauma-Informed Care Practices in Youth Residential Settings," University of South Florida College of Behavioral and Community Sciences, accessed August 11, 2021, www.trauma-informed-california.org/wp-content/uploads/2012/02/Organizational-Self-Assessment-for-Trauma-Informed-Care-Practices.pdf.

[10]"Trauma-Informed Organizational Capacity Scale," AIR, January 20, 2016, www.air.org/resource/framework-building-trauma-informed-organizations-and-systems.

[11]J. O. Prochaska and C. C. DiClemente, "Transtheoretical Therapy: Toward a More Integrative Model of Change," *Psychotherapy: Theory, Research & Practice* 19, no. 3 (1982): 276.

[12]"What We Know About How Child Sex Trafficking Happens," *Polaris* (blog), August 28, 2020, polarisproject.org/blog/2020/08/what-we-know-about-how-child-sex-trafficking-happens.

[13]*Trafficking in Persons Report: June 2018*, US Department of State, June 2018, www.state.gov/wp-content/uploads/2019/01/282798.pdf.

[14]Steve Corbett and Brian Fikkert, *When Helping Hurts: How to Alleviate Poverty Without Hurting the Poor . . . and Yourself* (Chicago: Moody Publishers, 2014).

[15]Adapted from Sandie Morgan, Dave Stachowiak, and Leonie Webster, "207—The Harms of Institutionalizing Children," *Ending Human Trafficking* podcast, September 22, 2019, endinghumantrafficking.org/podcast/207.

[16]*Self-Generated Child Sexual Abuse Material: Attitudes and Experiences*, Thorn, August 2020, info.thorn.org/hubfs/Research/08112020_SG-CSAM_AttitudesExperiences-Report_2019.pdf.

[17]*Self-Generated Child Sexual Abuse Material*, Thorn.

[18]*Responding to Online Threats: Minors' Perspectives on Disclosing, Reporting, and Blocking. Findings from 2020 Quantitative Research Among 9–17 Year Olds*, Thorn, May

2021, info.thorn.org/hubfs/Research/Responding%20to%20Online%20Threats_2021-Full-Report.pdf.

[19]*Responding to Online Threats*, Thorn.

[20]*Self-Generated Child Sexual Abuse Material*, Thorn.

[21]*Responding to Online Threats*, Thorn.

[22]"Sextortion Is an Emerging Form of Online Abuse," Thorn, 2021, www.thorn.org/sextortion.

[23]"The Issues: Sextortion," National Center for Missing and Exploited Children, 2021, www.missingkids.org/theissues/sextortion.

[24]John Shehan, quoted in Brenna O'Donnell, "COVID-19 and Missing & Exploited Children," *Missing Kids* (blog), April 30, 2021, www.missingkids.org/blog/2020/covid-19-and-missing-and-exploited-children.

[25]O'Donnell, "COVID-19 and Missing & Exploited Children."

[26]O'Donnell, "COVID-19 and Missing & Exploited Children."

[27]Sam Jones, "One in Every 122 People Is Displaced by War, Violence and Persecution, Says UN," *The Guardian*, June 18, 2015, www.theguardian.com/global-development/2015/jun/18/59m-people-displaced-war-violence-persecution-says-un.

[28]"1 Per Cent of Humanity Displaced: UNHCR Global Trends Reports," UN Refugee Agency, June 10, 2020, www.unhcr.org/en-us/news/press/2020/6/5ee9db2e4/1-cent-humanity-displaced-unhcr-global-trends-report.html.

[29]"Profile of Unauthorized Populations: United States," Migration Policy Institute, 2018, www.migrationpolicy.org/data/unauthorized-immigrant-population/state/US.

[30]"What Is a Refugee?," UN Refugee Agency, 2021, www.unrefugees.org/refugee-facts/what-is-a-refugee.

[31]"Challenges of Refugee Resettlement: Policy and Psychosocial Factors," National Association of Social Workers Social Justice Brief, 2019, www.socialworkers.org/LinkClick.aspx?fileticket=X2QaNfEuJUk%3D&portalid=0.

[32]"An Overview of U.S. Refugee Law and Policy," American Immigration Council, January 2020, www.americanimmigrationcouncil.org/research/overview-us-refugee-law-and-policy.

5. PROSECUTION

[1]John Cotton Richmond, "The Root Cause of Trafficking Is Traffickers," Human Trafficking Institute, January 31, 2017, www.traffickinginstitute.org/the-root-cause-of-trafficking-is-traffickers.

[2]Richmond, "The Root Cause."

[3]Sandie Morgan, Dave Stachowiak, and Victor Boutros, "228—Human Trafficking Institute Analyzes Federal Human Trafficking Criminal and Civil Prosecutions," *Ending Human Trafficking* podcast, July 12, 2020, endinghumantrafficking.org/podcast/228.

[4]Morgan, Stachowiak, and Boutros, "228—Human Trafficking Institute."

[5]"Cebu, the Philippines: Project Lantern Results Summary," International Justice Mission, March 2007, www.ijm.org/documents/studies/Cebu-Project-Lantern-Results-Summary.pdf.

[6]Adapted from Sandie Morgan, Dave Stachowiak, and Juliet Oliver, "221—Keys to Successful Prosecution," *Ending Human Trafficking* podcast, April 6, 2020, ending humantrafficking.org/podcast/221.

[7]Lauren Williams, "Man Faces O.C. Pimping Charges, Again," *Orange County Register*, July 26, 2016, www.ocregister.com/2016/07/26/man-faces-oc-pimping-charges-again.

[8]Greg Hardesty, "Case of 13-Year-Old Sex Trafficking Victim Sadly Isn't Unusual in Orange County, Officials Say," Behind the Badge, May 5, 2018, behindthebadge.com /case-13-year-old-sex-trafficking-victim-sadly-isnt-unusual-orange-county-officials-say.

[9]Viktoria Kristiansoon and Charlene Whitman-Barr, "Integrating a Trauma-Informed Response in Violence Against Women and Human Trafficking Prosecution," *Strategies*, February 2015, aequitasresource.org/wp-content/uploads/2018/09/Integrating-A-Trauma -Informed-Response-In-VAW-and-HT-Strategies.pdf.

[10]Adapted from Sandra Morgan, Dave Stachowiak, John Cotton Richmond, and Victor Boutros, "137—Interview with Prosecutors: John Cotton Richmond & Victor Boutros," *Ending Human Trafficking* podcast, January 16, 2017, endinghumantrafficking.org /podcast/137.

[11]"The Mission," Human Trafficking Institute, accessed June 9, 2021, www.trafficking institute.org/what-we-do.

[12]Gary Haugen, *Terrify No More* (Nashville: W Publishing Group, 2005), 241.

[13]Haugen, *Terrify No More*, 241.

6. PARTNERSHIP

[1]Todd L. Ely, Katie Edwards, Rachel Hogg Graham, and Danielle Varda, "Using Social Network Analysis to Understand the Perceived Role and Influence of Foundations," *The Foundation Review* 12, no. 1 (2020).

[2]Adapted from Sandie Morgan, Dave Stachowiak, and Erin Albright, "210—Collaboration: There Will Be Challenges," *Ending Human Trafficking* podcast, November 4, 2019, endinghumantrafficking.org/podcast/210.

[3]Adapted from Sandie Morgan, Dave Stachowiak, and Helen Sworn, "186—Building a Coalition and Building Capacity," *Ending Human Trafficking* podcast, December 2, 2018, endinghumantrafficking.org/podcast/186.

8. PRAYER

[1]Oswald Chambers, *My Utmost for His Highest*, ed. James Reimann rev. ed. (Grand Rapids, MI: Our Daily Bread Publishing, 2017), October 17 entry.

[2]Chambers, *My Utmost for His Highest*.

[3]Adam Hochschild, *Bury the Chains: Prophets and Rebels in the Fight to Free an Empire's Slaves* (Boston: First Mariner Books, 2006).

APPENDIX A: COMMON ABBREVIATIONS AND GLOSSARY

[1]Noreen Muhib, "Glossary of Human-Trafficking Acronyms and Terms," ABA Task Force on Human Trafficking, American Bar Association, January 1, 2013, www

.americanbar.org/groups/judicial/publications/judges_journal/2013/winter/glossary_of_humantrafficking_acronyms_and_terms.

APPENDIX C: FAITH AND FREEDOM POLICY BRIEF

[1]J. Frame, M. Tuckey, L. White, and E. Tomalin, *Faith and Freedom: The Role of Local Faith Actors in Anti–Modern Slavery and Human Trafficking—A Scoping Study* (Washington, DC: Joint Learning Initiative on Faith and Local Communities: Anti–Human Trafficking and Modern Slavery Hub, 2019), jliflc.com/resources/ams-ht-scoping-study.

ADDITIONAL RESOURCES

1. ELEMENTS AND TYPES OF HUMAN TRAFFICKING

"How Many Slaves Work for You?" Made in a Free World, accessed June 13, 2021, slaveryfootprint.org.

"Human Trafficking at Home: Labor Trafficking of Domestic Workers," Polaris and National Domestic Workers Alliance, polarisproject.org/wp-content/uploads/2019/09/Human_Trafficking_at_Home_Labor_Trafficking_of_Domestic_Workers.pdf.

"Human Trafficking at Home: Trafficking of Domestic Workers in the United States," Polaris, accessed June 13, 2021, polarisproject.org/wp-content/uploads/2019/07/Domestic_Worker_Fact_Sheet.pdf.

"Human Trafficking 101," Blue Campaign, Department of Homeland Security, accessed June 13, 2021, www.dhs.gov/sites/default/files/publications/ht_101_one-pager_.pdf.

"Is It Human Trafficking? You Might Be Surprised," Polaris, accessed June 13, 2021, polarisproject.org/wp-content/uploads/2019/07/Is_it_Human_Trafficking.pdf.

"Labor Trafficking Awareness" (videos), Blue Campaign, Department of Homeland Security, February 22, 2021, www.dhs.gov/blue-campaign/videos/labor-trafficking.

Laura J. Lederer, "Could Bringing Manufacturing Home Also Help Eradicate Modern Day Slavery?" *The Hill*, May 8, 2020, thehill.com/opinion/civil-rights/496573-could-bringing-manufacturing-home-also-help-eradicate-modern-day-slavery.

Laura J. Lederer, *Modern Slavery: A Documentary and Reference Guide* (Westport, CT: Greenwood, 2018).

"What Is Human Trafficking? Infographic," Blue Campaign, Department of Homeland Security, accessed June 13, 2021, www.dhs.gov/blue-campaign/infographic.

Sex Trafficking

Rebecca Bender, *In Pursuit of Love: One Woman's Journey from Trafficked to Triumphant* (Grand Rapids, MI: Zondervan, 2020).

Mary Frances Bowley, *The White Umbrella: Walking with Survivors of Sex Trafficking* (Chicago: Moody Publishers, 2012).

"Fact Sheet: Sex Trafficking," International Justice Mission, 2010, www.ijm.org/sites/default/files/download/resources/Factsheet-Sex-Trafficking.pdf.

Laura J. Lederer, "Addressing Demand: Utilizing Law and Law Enforcement to Target Customers of Commercial Sexual Exploitation," *Regent University Law Review* 23, no. 297 (2011): www.regent.edu/acad/schlaw/student_life/studentorgs/lawreview/docs/issues/v23n2/02Ledererv ol.23.2.pdf.

Laura J. Lederer and Christopher A. Wetzel, "The Health Consequences of Sex Trafficking and Their Implications for Identifying Victims in Healthcare Facilities," *Annals of Health Law* 23 (2014): www.icmec.org/wp-content/uploads/2015/10/Health-Consequences-of-Sex-Trafficking-and-Implications-for-Identifying-Victims-Lederer.pdf.

"The Life Story," NoVo Foundation, accessed June 13, 2021, thelifestory.org.

"Sex Trafficking Awareness" (videos), Blue Campaign, Department of Homeland Security, February 22, 2021, www.dhs.gov/blue-campaign/videos/sex-trafficking.

2. PAST AND PRESENT

"Human Trafficking Prevention: Bible Study/Small Group Guide," Faith Alliance Against Slavery and Trafficking, accessed June 13, 2021, mission14.org/assets/resources/downloads/Week_1_Joseph.pdf.

"Poverty and Human Trafficking," US Catholic Sisters Against Human Trafficking, accessed June 13, 2021, www.ipjc.org/wp-content/uploads/2016/09/USCSAHT%20-%20HT%20and%20Poverty.pdf.

Ben Reaoch, "Six Biblical Responses to Sex Trafficking," Radical, February 13, 2017, radical.net/articles/six-biblical-responses-to-sex-trafficking.

Roger Seth, "Bible Study: Joseph—Human Trafficking Survivor," Tearfund Learn, 2015, learn.tearfund.org/en/resources/publications/footsteps/footsteps_91-100/footsteps_96/bible_study_joseph_human_trafficking_survivor.

Trafficking in Persons Report 20th Edition, US Department of State, June 2020, www.state.gov/wp-content/uploads/2020/06/2020-TIP-Report-Complete-062420-FINAL.pdf.

"The 2019 Trafficking Victims Protection Reauthorization Act: A Topical Summary and Analysis of Four Bills," Polaris, 2019, polarisproject.org/wp-content/uploads/2020/01/Polaris-TVPRA-2019-Analysis.pdf.

3. PREVENTION

"Community Justice Assessment Tool for Churches," International Justice Mission, 2011, www.ijm.org/sites/default/files/download/resources/Community-Justice-Assessment-Tool.pdf.

"The Community Mapping Toolkit," Preston City Council, accessed June 13, 2021, ucanr.edu/sites/CA4-HA/files/206668.pdf.

"Ethical Storytelling Is a Community of Nonprofit Practitioners & Storytellers Learning How to Integrate a New Standard of Storytelling," Ethical Storytelling, accessed June 13, 2021, ethicalstorytelling.com.

Exodus Cry, "10 Big Myths About Prostitution," Moral Revolution, accessed August 14, 2021, www.moralrevolution.com/blog/10-big-myths-about-prostitution-exodus-cry.

"Free Template: Assessing the Needs of Your Community," Vanderbloemen, 2020, info.vanderbloemen.com/community-needs-assessment-for-churches-download.

"How Conspiracy Theorists Are Disrupting Efforts to Fight Human Trafficking," NPR, *Hear Every Voice* podcast, October 14, 2020, www.npr.org/2020/10/12/923019289/how-conspiracy-theorists-are-disrupting-efforts-to-fight-human-trafficking.

"Key Terms & Definitions," CTIP Program Management Office, accessed June 13, 2021, ctip.defense.gov/Portals/12/Documents/1%202_Key_Terms_and_Definitions_FINAL.pdf?ver=2015-04-08-114922-417.

"Language Matters," National Council for Mental Wellbeing, accessed June 13, 2021, www.thenationalcouncil.org/wp-content/uploads/2016/01/Attentive-FINAL-web.png.

Nikole Lim, *Liberation Is Here: Women Uncovering Hope in a Broken World* (Downers Grove, IL: InterVarsity Press, 2020).

"Myths and Facts About Human Trafficking," Office on Trafficking in Persons, US Department of Health and Human Services, accessed August 14, 2021, www.acf.hhs.gov/otip/about/myths-facts-human-trafficking.

"Myths, Facts, and Statistics," Polaris, 2021, polarisproject.org/myths-facts-and-statistics.

Alison Phillips, "The Sex Industry Wants to Keep You Confused About This" ," *Exodus Cry* blog, October 10, 2019, exoduscry.com/blog/changinglaws/the-sex-industry-wants-to-keep-you-confused-about-this.

Dawn Post, "Why Human Traffickers Prey on Foster-Care Kids," CityLimits, January 23, 2015, citylimits.org/2015/01/23/why-traffickers-prey-on-foster-care-kids.

"Poverty and Human Trafficking," U.S. Catholic Sisters Against Human Trafficking, accessed June 13, 2021, www.ipjc.org/wp-content/uploads/2016/09/USCSAHT%20-%20HT%20and%20Poverty.pdf.

"Recognizing Human Trafficking: Vulnerabilities & Signs of Recruitment," Polaris, 2021, polarisproject.org/recognizing-human-trafficking-vulnerabilities-recruitment.

"Runaway and Housing," The Life Story, accessed June 13, 2021, thelifestory.org/assets/downloads/about/handouts/en/TLS_Handouts_Runaway_Housing.pdf.

"Section 1. Developing a Plan for Assessing Local Needs and Resources," Community Tool Box, accessed June 13, 2021, ctb.ku.edu/en/table-of-contents/assessment/assessing-community-needs-and-resources/develop-a-plan/main.

"Sex Trafficking in the U.S.: A Closer Look at U.S. Citizen Victims," Polaris, accessed June 13, 2021, polarisproject.org/wp-content/uploads/2019/09/us-citizen-sex-trafficking.pdf.

"Slow Kingdom Coming Practices Tipsheet," Humanitarian Disaster Institute, Wheaton College, 2020, www.wheaton.edu/media/humanitarian-disaster-institute/Slow-Kingdom-Coming-Tip-Sheet.pdf.

United Nations Office on Drugs and Crime, *An Introduction to Human Trafficking: Vulnerability, Impact and Action* (New York: United Nations, 2008), www.unodc.org/documents/human-trafficking/An_Introduction_to_Human_Trafficking_-_Background_Paper.pdf.

4. PROTECTION

"Adverse Childhood Experiences," The Life Story, accessed June 13, 2021, thelifestory.org/assets/downloads/about/handouts/en/TLS_Handouts_ACE.pdf.

Kent Annan, *You Welcomed Me: Loving Refugees and Immigrants Because God First Loved Us* (Downers Grove, IL: InterVarsity Press, 2018).

"Engaging Parents and Guardians of High School-Aged Sons in Stopping Sexual Exploitation and Harm," Chicago Alliance Against Sexual Exploitation, accessed June 13, 2021, humantraffickinghotline.org/sites/default/files/Engaging%20Parents%20and%20Guardians%20of%20High%20School-Aged%20Sons.pdf.

"Fact Sheet: Identifying Victims of Human Trafficking," Office on Trafficking in Persons, US Department of Health & Human Services, accessed June 13, 2021, www.acf.hhs.gov/sites/default/files/orr/fact_sheet_identifying_victims_of_human_trafficking.pdf.

"How to Talk About Human Trafficking with Children and Adolescents," Baylor University, April 2, 2019, onlinegrad.baylor.edu/resources/conversations-human-trafficking-children-teens.

"Human Trafficking: Protecting Our Youth," US Department of Health and Human Services, 2018, www.childwelfare.gov/pubPDFs/trafficking_ts_2018.pdf.

"Immigration," The Life Story, accessed June 13, 2021, thelifestory.org/assets/downloads/about/handouts/en/TLS_Handouts_Immigration.pdf.

"Implementing a Trauma-Informed Approach," Office to Monitor and Combat Trafficking in Persons, US Department of State, www.state.gov/wp-content/uploads/2019/02/283795.pdf.

"Interviewing Tips for Health-care Practitioners," Toolkit to Combat Trafficking in Persons, United States Department of Health and Human Services, accessed June 13, 2021, www.unodc.org/documents/human-trafficking/Toolkit-files/08-58296_tool_6-9.pdf.

Sandie Morgan and Mark Kadel, "66—Refugee Resettlement, Reducing Risk for Human Trafficking," *Ending Human Trafficking* podcast, October 17, 2013, endinghumantrafficking.org/podcast/66.

"National Human Trafficking Hotline" (poster), Polaris, accessed June 13, 2021, humantraffickinghotline.org/sites/default/files/NationalHTHotline_Poster_English_0.pdf.

"10 Key Ingredients for Trauma-Informed Care," Trauma-Informed Care Implementation Resource Center, accessed June 13, 2021, www.traumainformedcare.chcs.org/wp-content/uploads/2018/11/Infographic-TIC.pdf.

"Trauma and Addiction," The Life Story, accessed June 13, 2021, thelifestory.org/assets/downloads/about/handouts/en/TLS_Handouts_Trauma_Addiction.pdf.

"2018 Prevention Resource Guide," US Department of Health and Human Services Administration for Children and Families, 2018, www.childwelfare.gov/pubPDFs/guide_2018.pdf.

2019 Data Report: The U.S. National Human Trafficking Hotline, Polaris, accessed June 13, 2021, polarisproject.org/wp-content/uploads/2019/09/Polaris-2019-US-National-Human-Trafficking-Hotline-Data-Report.pdf.

Bessel van der Kolk, *The Body Keeps the Score: Brain, Mind, and Body in the Healing of Trauma* (New York: Penguin, 2014).

"What to Expect when You Call the National Human Trafficking Hotline" (online training module), Polaris, accessed June 13, 2021, polarisproject.adobeconnect.com/_a983384736/p8gk0st7jmd.

5. PROSECUTION

"High School Curriculum," A21, accessed June 13, 2021, www2.a21.org/shop-offer.php?intid=365.

"High School Curriculum (Spanish)," A21, accessed June 13, 2021, www2.a21.org/shop-offer.php?intid=1065.

"How Local Police Can Combat the Global Problem of Human Trafficking," Police Executive Research Forum, August 2020, www.policeforum.org/assets/CombatHumanTrafficking.pdf.

"Human Trafficking Taskforce e-Guide," Office for Victims of Crime, US Department of Justice, accessed June 13, 2021, www.ovcttac.gov/taskforceguide/eguide.

"Law Enforcement," The Life Story, accessed June 13, 2021, thelifestory.org/assets/downloads/about/handouts/en/TLS_Handouts_LawEnforcement.pdf.

"Primary Prevention Program," A21, accessed June 13, 2021, www2.a21.org/shop-offer.php?intid=5141.

6. PARTNERSHIP

"Become an Abolitionist," Exodus Cry, 2021, exoduscry.com/abolitionist.

Engage Together, engagetogether.com/toolkits.

"Global Modern Slavery Directory," Polaris, accessed June 13, 2021, www.globalmodernslavery.org.

Shayne Moore, *Global Soccer Mom: Changing the World Is Easier Than You Think* (Grand Rapids, MI: Zondervan, 2016).

Shayne Moore and Kimberly McOwen Yim, *Refuse to Do Nothing: Finding Your Power to Abolish Modern-Day Slavery* (Downers Grove, IL: InterVarsity Press, 2013).

Speaker presentations from the Christian Abolitionists Symposium, Christian Abolitionists, October 10, 2018, instituteforsheltercare.org/christian-abolitionists.

7. POLICY

"Advocacy Toolkit: A Roots Guide," Tearfund Learn, 2015, learn.tearfund.org/en/resources/series/roots-guides/advocacy-toolkit--a-roots-guide.

"Becoming a Church that Cares Well for the Abused" (training curriculum), ChurchCares.com, 2019, churchcares.com.

GRACE: Godly Response to Abuse in the Christian Environment, netgrace.org.

"Lies Traffickers Tell" (poster), Tearfund Learn, 2015, learn.tearfund.org/en/resources/publications/footsteps/footsteps_91-100/footsteps_96/lies_traffickers_tell.

"The Samaritan Women Training," The Samaritan Women Institute for Shelter Care, 2021, thesamaritanwomen.org/training.

8. PRAYER

"Abolishing Injustice in the 21st Century Prayer Guide," A21, 2013, aheartforjustice.com/wp-content/uploads/2010/08/a21-prayer-guide.pdf.

"Prayer Guide for the Abolition of Slavery," International Justice Mission, accessed June 13, 2021, aheartforjustice.com/wp-content/uploads/2010/08/ijm-prayer-guide-for-the-abolition-of-slavery.pdf.

"Prayer Guide for the Victims of Sex Trafficking," The Salvation Army, accessed June 13, 2021, aheartforjustice.com/wp-content/uploads/2010/08/salvation-army-prayer-guide.pdf.

"72 Daily Prayer Points," A Heart for Justice, accessed June 13, 2021, aheartforjustice.com/wp-content/uploads/2012/08/72DailyPrayerPoints.pdf.

"She Is Priceless Devotional," accessed June 13, 2021, aheartforjustice.com/wp-content/uploads/2010/08/Priceless_Devotional.pdf.

INDEX